Asperger Syndrome and Adolescence

Practical Solutions for School Success

Asperger Syndrome and Adolescence

Practical Solutions for School Success

Brenda Smith Myles
Diane Adreon

With Jennifer Stella

AAPC

Autism Asperger Publishing Company
P.O. Box 2373
Shawnee Mission, Kansas 66283-0173

© 2001 by Autism Asperger Publishing Co.
P.O. Box 23173
Shawnee Mission, Kansas 66283-0173

Publisher's Cataloging-in-Publication
(provided by Quality Books, Inc.)

Myles, Brenda
    Asperger syndrome and adolescence :
practical solutions for school success
/ [Brenda Smith Myles, Diane Adreon] – 1st ed.
    p. cm.
    Includes bibliographic references and index.
    Library of Congress Control Number: 2001 132003
    ISBN: 0-9672514-9-4

    1. Autistic children–Education.
2. Asperger's syndrome
I. Adreon, Diane. II. Title.

LC4717.M95 2001   371.94
               QBI01-200062

This book is designed in Garamond and Techno

Managing Editor: Kirsten McBride
Cover Design: Taku Hagiwara
Production Assistant: Ginny Biddulph
Interior Design/Production: Tappan Design

Printed in the United States of America

*This book is dedicated to
John Oak, Jeffrey Schmidt
and CJ Briggs —
Our hope for the future*

TABLE OF CONTENTS

CHAPTER 1

Middle and High School Experiences for the Neurotypical Adolescent

Authored with Jennifer Stella

Moving from elementary school to middle school and middle school to high school are harrowing experiences for many young neurotypical youths because of the changes they face on many fronts – personal as well as academic. Structural changes that include a larger school with departmentalized teaching worry many students. Concerns about doing well or simply being able to "make it" also prevail. As teachers begin to group students by ability and infuse competition as a motivator, particularly in high school, students report having difficulty living up to adults' expectations. As a result, some students show marked losses in achievement when they move into middle and high school, specifically in science, social studies, and reading (Adreon & Stella, 2001; Alspaugh, 1998). In addition, students themselves report that they feel less competent than in elementary school. For example, they are less confident that they have or can develop the math and English skills they need to survive secondary school (Anderman & Midgley, 1997; Wigfield & Eccles, 1994).

Concurrently, social expectations increase and peer relationships become more complex around this age. Moving beyond the "safe" and familiar confines of family and elementary school, adolescents are required to interact with a larger, more diverse student body and a broader community, which places greater demands on social competence. As a result, students who lack social skills often experience significant adjustment problems and feelings of negative self-worth during this transition (Shoffner & Williamson, 2000). As if all of this wasn't enough, students must also cope with the physiological changes associated with the onset of puberty (Adreon & Stella, 2001).[1]

For these reasons, many adolescents moving into middle and high school suffer from great psychological stress, teetering between childhood and something akin to greater maturity. No wonder, then, that many kids simply get lost during this transition. Debra-Lynn Hook (2000), the parent of a middle school student, described it best:

> Middle school is where kids float for years, groundless and unnoticed, between thinking they're supposed to be all grown up and secretly wishing they could sit on the floor and play tiddlywinks, even as they tote 200 pounds of books on their prepubescent backs between classes. (pp. H-1, H-8)

This period is so difficult that many youths complain about the stress they feel (Gerler, Drew, & Mohr, 1990). The combination of the varied stressors outlined above leaves many students feeling unsettled and overwhelmed. As a result, some of them begin a serious downward spiral during the transition to middle school. The purported causes include lack of skills to negotiate complex social mores and increased self-doubt as students see themselves judged by the grades they obtain (Black, 1999). Of the stressors described by young people themselves, some seem minor on the surface (worry that they don't know how to open a locker or won't be able to make it to the next class in time if it is located in another wing of the school), while others seem monumental (concern about getting good grades to meet long-range educational goals). Table 1.1 includes a list of what middle and high school students have identified as specific stressors during this time of their lives.

In addition to student-identified concerns, teachers of middle and high school students have also observed a number of stressors

---

[1]Because of space constraints, and because they fall outside the specific focus of this book, two issues of extreme importance in adolescense – sexuality and planning the transition to adulthood – will not be addressed here.

Table 1.1
Concerns Voiced by Neurotypical Students in Middle and High School

Getting lost in school

Figuring out and following a complex schedule

Being late to class

Finding and opening the locker

Remembering what class to go to next

Getting through the crowded halls to arrive in class on time

Finding the bathrooms

Finding the lunchroom

Figuring out the lunchroom routine

Having to deal with several teachers

Coping with different rules and routines across classes

Being "picked on" by teachers

Difficulty understanding classroom material

Difficulty meeting academic demands

Keeping up with and organizing classroom materials

Finishing heavy homework assignments

Making low grades

Feeling that they can't handle additional responsibilities

Worrying that there is no one to provide help when needed

Worrying generally about "making it through" middle or high school

Feeling alone or isolated

Being alienated from other students

Being lonely and unpopular

Teasing and mistreatment by older students

Worrying that school failures will not allow them to achieve long-range goals

Being unable to find the right bus to go home

Note. Items from Arowosafe & Irvin (1992); Black (1999); Hartos & Power (1997); Mizelle (1990); Mullins & Irvin (2000); Odegaard & Heath (1992); Phelan, Yu, & Davidson (1994); Schumacher (1998); Weldy (1995).

among their students. Many overlap with those expressed by students; others have not appeared on student-generated lists. But this does not negate their reality. Instead, these may be significant stressors that have not been voiced by youths for some reason. Exposure to peer pressure, understanding cliques, and having to accept more responsibility for their actions are but a few of the stressors teachers think have a major impact on the academic success and general well-being of adolescents (see Table 1.2).

But all is not as bleak as it appears here. While there is no doubt that students experience numerous stressors related to the transition to middle and high school, many of them are balanced by positive events that students are eagerly awaiting. These include environmental changes such as eating in the cafeteria and moving between classrooms, as well as opportunities to become independent decision makers and problem solvers (see Table 1.3). In addition, for the neurotypical youth, even the more "serious" stressors are generally short-term and manageable. For example, watching an older student go

---

Table 1.2
Teachers' Perceptions of the Concerns
of Students in Middle and High School

Changing classes
Diminishing parent involvement
Coping with more teachers
Having no recess, no free time in or between classes
Adjusting to new grading standards and procedures
Exposure to more peer pressure
Cliquishness
Fearing a new, larger, more impersonal school
Accepting more responsibility for their actions
Dealing with older children
Merging with students from numerous elementary schools
Coping with unrealistic parental expectations
Having little experience with extracurricular classes
Unfamiliarity with student lockers
Following the school schedule
Scheduling for and completing longer-range assignments

Note. Items from Weldy cited in Schumacher (1998).

through the steps of the lunchroom routine a couple of times is usually enough for the typical youth to understand the routine and therefore quickly alleviates any stress and anxiety stemming from this new experience. The same goes for finding one's way around the school, which soon becomes routine. Other new experiences may require a longer adjustment period, such as budgeting adequate time for homework and understanding the cliquishness that often prevails in middle and high school. However, even here the neurotypical adolescent gradually adjusts.

But this book is not about the typical adolescent! It is about adolescents with Asperger Syndrome (AS), who often experience difficulties acclimating to new school situations due to some of their defining characteristics. How does a youth with AS feel about and cope with this new culture called middle school and high school?

Jonathan, a 13-year-old boy with AS, summed up his feelings about middle and high school in a telling, matter-of-fact way. When asked by his mother what he was looking forward to in middle school, Jonathan replied, "The end."

Whereas a growing number of books have been written on younger children, we are focusing on a critical stage in the life of a person with AS. During adolescence some of the most salient characteristics of AS are often accentuated, leading to serious academic and social problems.

Table 1.3
What Students Look Forward to as
They Enter Middle and High School

Getting their own lockers
Having different teachers for several different subjects
Moving to different rooms for various classes
Eating in the cafeteria
Participating in a more complete athletic program
Having more choices about what classes to take
Being able to have more control or make their own decisions
Making new friends

Note. Items from Arowosafe & Irvin (1992); Odegaard & Heath (1992).

This book provides suggestions and strategies intended to make the transition to and survival in middle and high school easier for the adolescent with AS. We begin with an overview of the characteristics of AS that often make the adolescent school years particularly difficult. School-based assessment methods, general supports, and transition strategies for youths with AS are then described to help parents, educators, and students themselves reduce the trauma and distress associated with adolescence. The last two chapters consist of "real-life" experiences. Parents and adolescents share the successes and challenges experienced by teens with AS in Chapter 6 and in Chapter 7 a case study illustrates how the strategies in this book were combined to provide a successful school experience for an adolescent with AS.

CHAPTER 2

Asperger Syndrome: Characteristics Impacting the Middle and High School Years

In recent years, Asperger Syndrome (AS) has been recognized as a diagnosis that affects approximately 1 in every 200 to 250 individuals (Kadesjo, Gillberg, & Hagberg, 1999). Because it impacts so many people, researchers and practitioners have made great efforts to identify and develop strategies that can facilitate school and home success. However, most of this work has focused on young children at the elementary school level, with little attention to how to help youth with AS as they transition into middle and high school.

In this chapter we will discuss the characteristics of AS that have the greatest impact during the adolescent and teen years. The discussion is grouped around five major areas: cognitive, language and social issues, sensory issues, behavior, and motor skills.

Cognition

Intelligence

Individuals with AS typically have average to above-average IQ. However, a larger percent of persons with AS have IQs that are considered to be superior or very superior to what is seen in the general population. Unlike individuals with nonverbal learning disabilities, they usually do not manifest a large difference between performance and verbal scores on intelligence tests (Barnhill, Hagiwara, Myles, & Simpson, 2000).

Why is having an average to above-average intelligence a problem for middle and high school students? Those who do not understand the unique characteristics of Asperger Syndrome think that IQ is the best determiner of school ability and functioning. Therefore, they cannot understand why a youth with an IQ of 140 has trouble getting her homework home, becomes anxious over a schedule change, or does not follow a multistep direction.

Maturity

The emotional maturity level of adolescents with AS and other neurological difficulties is significantly below what is expected for their chronological age. Particularly during the teen years, students with AS may appear to have the emotional maturity of someone two-thirds their age. Maturity is often assessed by actions in social situations. To be socially adept, we must be able to perceive and understand social clues such as frowns, smiles, boredom, emotions, and so on. And we must be able to think clearly about our own behavior and the behavior of others. In addition, maturity involves conforming to the behavioral and social expectations of peers.

These are all areas of great difficulty for individuals with AS, who often appear "clueless" or "naïve," failing to understand the subtle interactions of peers or know how to fit in (Myles & Southwick, 1999). Their interests, too, may mark them as immature. Obsession with Pokemon,™ while perfectly acceptable in grade school, is not considered appropriate by most typical teens.

Rote Memory

The ability to commit to memory various and sundry facts common among many individuals with AS can be an asset. For example, this skill often makes them sought after in quiz bowls, and geography and spelling bees, where they use their vast registry of information to recall little-known facts or to spell words that few of us know even exist.

But rote memory can be misleading. Superior factual recall often gives the impression that adolescents with AS understand the concepts they are talking about. But, in reality, they may not. Typically, the person with Asperger Syndrome picks up from text or conversation certain words or phrases that appeal to him for some reason and uses them in a rote manner that mimics comprehension. It is this parroting that often gives the impression that the person has well-developed higher-level comprehension skills, whereas comprehension is only at the factual level. That is, he may be able to answer multiple-choice questions on a worksheet about a novel he has read, but be unable to understand the main character's motivation.

Rote memory skills also lead to the false impression that students can remember pieces of information or events at any time. Often individuals with AS store the facts in such a way that they cannot retrieve them unless a specific word or term is used as a prompt. Open-ended questions such as "What did I tell you to do the next time Jim called you a name" may not trigger a response because the student has stored the information under "name calling" and did not associate it specifically with Jim.

Theory-of-Mind Deficits

How individuals with Asperger Syndrome view the world and interpret events around them sometimes differs from the way their peers and teachers interpret them. Part of this difficulty is associated with what we assume about thinking. Neurotypical peers tend to believe that others know what they are thinking in a given situation and that they do not need to spell things out in detail to be understood. When Mark turns to his friend Ed to say, "Awesome," Mark assumes that Ed knows he is referring to Jennifer, the cute blonde who just passed by. Ed, in turn, also knows at that point that he should probably not try to make Jennifer his girlfriend, as Mark obviously has his eyes on her, and that it would probably work if instead he tried to become good friends with Jennifer's best friend, Monique. All this is communicated with just one word, "awesome."

The ability to pick up and act on such assumptions is referred to as "theory of mind." Cumine, Leach and Stevenson (1998) define theory of mind as "the ability to think about other people's thinking – and further, to think about what they think about our thinking – and, even further to think about what they think we think about their thinking and so on ..." (p. 19). This is a problem for all individuals with AS and may be a particularly troublesome issue for adolescents. When we talk to someone, we try to read her mind to see if she is interested in the topic of conversation. This mind reading includes looking at facial expression, body stance, and voice tone and determining whether there is match or mismatch among them.

Adolescents generally consider themselves to be masters of subtlety. They often act cool or disinterested when, in actuality, they are excited or fascinated. A subtle nod might be used to greet the closest friend. It seems that adolescents have a verbal and nonverbal language of their own. As a result, teens with AS who don't know this language often don't fit in socially. The wrong type of greeting, talking to a teacher under "inappropriate circumstances" (this includes viewing the teacher as a person!), or ignoring a subtle communication from a peer can instantly place a peer in social jeopardy – a status that may not easily be overcome. But it is not only peer interactions that require the use of theory-of-mind skills. At the middle and high school levels, the six or seven teachers who teach the student with AS require that he figure out the teachers' often unstated expectations.

Executive Function

Adolescents with AS have problems with executive function. That is, they have trouble with planning, organizing, shifting attention, and multitasking. Many middle and high school homework assignments are long-term, including lengthy reading assignments, research, preparation of a model and culminating in writing a paper. Most students create a timeline that will allow them to complete all tasks by the due date. But teens with AS often do not know how to approach a complex task. They don't know how to break it down into manageable parts and budget their time accordingly. Often they spend an inordinate amount of time talking or worrying about a long-term project without beginning the task. They see the project as an amorphous assignment that they simply cannot accomplish.

Knowing how to systematically approach a task is also problematic for many students with AS. Billy Joe was given a long-term assignments on satellites. As a part of this project he was to identify a specific satellite and write a paper on it using at least five references, including a picture. Billy Joe chose to write the paper first and then look for a picture of the satellite. Unfortunately, using this approach, he had to redo his paper because he could not find a picture of the particular satellite he had chosen. Most adolescents know to scan an assignment to make sure they have included essential information. In this example, neurotypical students would know to look for the picture before writing the paper to be sure they had everything they needed and, if not, adjust their plans.

> **Most students with AS also have organizational problems. They have no system for determining which papers are important.**

Such difficulties in starting a task are compounded by problems in seeking assistance. Billy Joe experienced countless problems with his satellite project. Deciding to use the Internet as one resource, he spent three hours trying to find information on satellites. Each time he keyed in the term "satellite," he found information on retail satellite offices. He even tried several search engines using the term. It wasn't until his mother asked how his project was progressing that he told her, or anybody else, that he could not find any information on satellites in space. His anxiety level, at this point, was high because of his many unsuccessful attempts. If his mother had not intervened, he just would have continued searching using ineffective means.

Most students with AS also have organizational problems. They do homework but cannot find it in their backpack when they are ready to turn it in. They have no system for keeping textbooks and notebooks together or for determining which papers are important to keep or which can be discarded. Moreover, they often don't have the proper supplies for class because they can't find pencils or paper.

Further, attention shifting is difficult for many students with AS. They don't know, for example, how to shift their attention from completing individual work to listening to the teacher giving a new direction to the group. While Shayna is copying homework from the board, she cannot shift her attention to listen to the teacher who is providing additional information about the homework assignment. She will be ready to listen only after she has copied the assignment.

For this reason, multitasking is difficult. Students with AS need to complete one task before beginning another. They often have difficulty leaving a task unfinished to begin a second assignment.

Problem Solving

Many describe the problem-solving skills of adolescents with AS as erratic. When they are in the process of investigating an area of special interest, they may show highly developed problem-solving skills. But in day-to-day tasks, they often demonstrate ineffective problem solving or appear to lack such skills entirely. On the other hand, some students with AS learn one problem-solving strategy and use it consistently regardless of the situation or outcome. For example, if the school locker does not open, the student may nevertheless keep trying the same combination over and over. Although the strategy is sometimes effective, if the student has tried the correct locker combination five times in a row unsuccessfully, chances are that there is another problem with the locker. However, many students with AS do not know the problem-solving strategy that involves asking an adult or peer for help when difficulty arises and alternate options become necessary (Myles & Southwick, 1999).

Difficulty accessing information or strategies at the right time makes problem solving even more difficult. Although the student may be able to recite several problem-solving strategies and name situations to which they can be generalized, he may not be able to recall any of these strategies when they are needed. By the time the student cognitively realizes that a problem exists, he is typically so confused, angry or disoriented that his reaction becomes behavioral – a tantrum or withdrawal.

Problem-solving becomes particularly difficult in academics if abstract concepts are involved. Thus, adolescents with Asperger Syndrome frequently have difficulty with word problems, estimation, algebra, and geometry – all of which require problem-solving skills and often contain a high level of abstraction.

Generalization

As mentioned, individuals with AS often have problems applying information and skills across settings and persons as well as integrating learned material and experiences. While students may memorize sets of facts, such lists often remain unconnected bits of information. For example, they may be able to cite a rule or set of procedures that they are to follow in a given situation, but be incapable of applying them when needed. Teachers often misinterpret this lack of symmetry between verbalization and actions as intentional misbehavior on the part of the student with AS, thereby missing an important characteristic of AS.

The situation is exacerbated when the student experiences stress and anxiety. Information known when not under stress is often not available in a difficult situation. In these cases, the student with AS is likely to revert back to behavior learned early on, which is not typically appropriate (i.e., pacing back and forth, refusing to listen coupled with "you can't make me" remarks, hitting others). And when the stress and anxiety are gone, the skill reappears as if by magic. The behaviors are also gone. But the damage has been done – the student failed to provide the correct answer and demonstrated inappropriate behavior causing peers to poke fun.

Special Interests

Although the unique absorption in special interests found among individuals with AS has been widely acknowledged, little has been done to turn them into viable life or vocational skills. For example, an intense preoccupation with the weather could point in the direction of a career in meteorology. One reason why we are reluctant to make that connection is that we have difficulty determining whether the special interest will turn out to be such a preoccupation that it will prevent the child from engaging in other activities (Howlin, 1998) – known as a "primary obsession" – or whether it is a secondary interest that can be a motivator but is not all-encompassing (Myles & Simpson, 1998).

Marta's special interest is photocopy machines. She knows the makes and models of all existing machines and can disassemble them rapidly. Marta's parents and teachers consider this a primary obsession. If someone mentions "photocopy machine," Marta starts talking rapidly about the topic and ends up frantically searching for a particular machine to discuss and perhaps disassemble. Her parents and teachers have tried to discourage others from talking about the topic to prevent this behavior.

Harry, on the other had, has a secondary special interest in photocopiers. Although he enjoys talking about them, he knows how to regulate his behavior. When given parameters for talking about photocopy machines, he can follow them. For example, when Harry meets his social and academic goals during the day, he is given time to do research on photocopiers or discuss them with a peer or adult. When the allotted time for research or discussion ends, he can easily transition to a new task.

Another reason why special interests are often not capitalized on in school is their individual nature. That is, addressing an adolescent's special interest often requires altering the curriculum and coordinating activities among teachers – a time-consuming proposition for many middle and high school teachers, who see over 100 young people each day. One additional reason is given for not focusing curricula around a particular topic – the often transient nature of special interests. In order to motivate Jeri to participate in language arts, Mrs. Johnson developed an individual nine-week unit around Egypt, Jeri's special interest. The unit contained all of the competencies that the other students would meet during this period. One week into the individualized unit, Jeri decided that she was no longer interested in Egypt and her motivation for completing the study guide was gone. In fact, at this point, the unit became aversive to her.

Language and Socialization Issues

Many adolescents with Asperger Syndrome have good structural language skills, such as clear pronunciation and correct syntax, but poor pragmatic communication abilities that negatively impact their ability to get along with others. This is particularly problematic during adolescence, because socialization with peers is often the primary motivator at this age. Social interactions are complex and may seem contradictory. Communication at this stage is all about subtlety and getting along with the peer group.

John, a neurotypical student, really likes school but knows that it is not acceptable to voice this opinion unless he wants to be considered a geek. So he keeps this to himself while loudly proclaiming to his "cool" friends that "school is really dumb." At the same time, however, John knows how to communicate his interest in school to his teachers in a subtle way. While he infrequently volunteers to answer questions – for fear of exposing himself to his peers – when directly asked a question in class, he always responds with the correct answer. His friends know that John is smart but like him anyway because he knows how not to act overly smart.

The student with AS would not understand this simple, subtle communication and might commit the serious error of volunteering to answer all the questions he knew the answer to. This faux pas would be compounded when he showed a degree of excitement about knowing a particular response. The "cool" student would never raise his hand, wave it in front of the teacher, and say, "Please, please, call on me!"

Social deficits that typically cause problems for adolescents with AS include the following:

1. **Lack of understanding that nonverbal cues such as facial expressions, gestures, proximity, and eye contact convey meaning and attitudes.** Students with AS miss out on many social opportunities because they do not "get" the important parts of communication. That is, they often cannot read facial expressions, gestures, and so forth. Johnny, a student with AS, notices that Katie, a girl in several of his classes, frequently glances over at him and smiles. Johnny does not realize that these signs might indicate that Katie likes him. Similarly, Juan often gets in trouble in science class because he doesn't read his teacher's nonverbal cues. As a warning, the teacher often gives the "teacher look," which Juan does not see or understand. So he does not calm down or attend like everyone else in the class when "the look" occurs.

2. **Difficulty using language to initiate or maintain a conversation.** Although extremely verbal, students with AS often do not know how to approach others or carry on a conversation. This situation becomes worse when stress and anxiety are added. Mark and Craig are in the school hall conversing. Sean, a teen

with AS, walks up to them and begins rocking back and forth, waiting for the opportunity to join in the conversation. Sean's rocking is a sign that he is anxious to talk but does not know when or how to join in. As a result, his friends continue ignoring Sean's nonverbal overtures to be a part of the conversation.

Yet, adults often report that adolescents with AS are competent communicators. This is because many adults don't take into account how they compensate for the problems adolescents with AS experience. That is, adults will tolerate a conversation on an uninteresting topic (i.e., hurricanes) and will actually ask questions on the topic. Also, adults will adjust for proximity, allow the student "thinking time," and tolerate it when the student refuses to change topic.

As the environment becomes more complex, involving many people, noise, and other stimuli, the social and language skills of the adolescent with AS seem to deteriorate. For example, Mrs. Rice, the language arts teacher, is confused by Tara's inconsistency in social and language skills. Before school, when the two of them are alone, Tara and Mrs. Rice had a fairly complex conversation about Greek myths. Mrs. Rice felt that Tara demonstrated good language comprehension and social skills. However, at the end of language arts class, Tara did not get her homework planner signed by Mrs. Rice. She did walk up near the teacher's desk waiting for the opportunity to ask Mrs. Rice to sign the planner. But she was unable to ask her question because other students were asking questions, too. When the bell rang signaling the end of class, Tara took that as her cue to leave. So she left without getting her planner signed because she didn't know how to enter into the conversation.

3. **A tendency to interpret words or phrases concretely.** Adolescents with AS often are extremely literal. Mr. Thomas thinks that Tim is a "smart aleck" because of the way he responds in class. One day, when Mr. Thomas asked Tim if he had the time, Tim merely said yes. He did not realize that Mr. Thomas was actually asking what time it was.

4. **Difficulty realizing that other people's perspective in conversation must be considered.** Problems in this area often lead to one-sided monologues without monitoring whether the listener is interested or not. A group of middle school girls were over-

head talking between classes. As Lori, a girl with AS, rounded the corner, Nicole said to her friends, "Don't even look at her or slow down because she will start talking about Egypt and dead mummies. She doesn't know that we could care less."

Problems in perspective include not knowing when it is appropriate to talk about a topic. Nick, who was interested in anatomy, couldn't understand why his peers were not fascinated by his lunchtime discussion of the gory details of his neighbor's dog's internal organs spilling out after it had been run over by a car. To Nick, seeing the intestines was extremely interesting.

5. **Failure to understand the unstated rules of the hidden curriculum or the set of rules that everyone knows, but that has not been directly taught.** This includes knowing (a) what to say and to whom, (b) how to dress, (c) how to act, and (d) how to differentiate gentle teasing from bullying. Youth with AS either monopolize the conversation or converse minimally with others. In addition, they may show abnormalities in inflection and repeat phrases inappropriately and out of context.

6. **Lack of awareness that what you say to a given person in one conversation may impact how that individual interacts with you in the future.** Nancy, a high school student, saw herself as being helpful when she told Maureen, a neurotypical peer, that the horizontal lines on her shirt made her look fat. Nancy was not trying to hurt Maureen's feelings; she was merely stating a fact as she saw it. Therefore, she was totally surprised at Maureen's cold look and lack of response later on in the day when they met again.

Sensory Issues

Although research in AS and sensory integration is limited to date, it has been documented that children and youth with AS have sensory problems that make them appear similar to cognitively challenged children with autism (Dunn, Myles, & Orr, in press; Rinner, 2000). In fact, children with AS may have marked issues in each of the seven sensory areas: (a) tactile, (b) vestibular, (c) proprioceptive, (d) visual, (e) auditory, (f) gustatory, and (g) olfactory (see Table 2.1 for a definition and illustration of these terms).

Table 2.1
Descriptions of the Sensory Systems

System	Location	Function
Tactile (touch)	**Skin** – density of cell distribution varies throughout the body. Areas of greatest density include mouth, hands, and genitals.	Provides information about the environment and object qualities (touch, pressure, texture, hard, soft, sharp, dull, heat, cold, pain).
Vestibular (balance)	**Inner ear** – stimulated by head movements and input from other senses, especially visual.	Provides information about where our body is in space, and whether or not we or our surroundings are moving. Tells about speed and direction of movement.
Proprioception (body awareness)	**Muscles and joints** – activated by muscle contractions and movement.	Provides information about where a certain body part is and how it is moving.
Visual (sight)	**Retina of the eye** – stimulated by light.	Provides information about objects and persons. Helps us define boundaries as we move through time and space.
Auditory (hearing)	**Inner ear** – stimulated by air/sound waves.	Provides information about sounds in the environment (loud, soft, high, low, near, far).
Gustatory (taste)	**Chemical receptors in the tongue** – closely entwined with the olfactory (smell) system.	Provides information about different types of taste (sweet, sour, bitter, salty, spicy).
Olfactory (smell)	**Chemical receptors in the nasal structure** – closely associated with the gustatory system.	Provides information about different types of smell (musty, acrid, putrid, flowery, pungent).

From *Asperger Syndrome and Sensory Issues: Practical Solutions for Making Sense of the World* (p. 5), by B. S. Myles, K. T. Cook, N. E. Miller, L. Rinner, and L. A. Robbins, 2000. Shawnee Mission, KS: AAPC. Reprinted by permission.

In addition to the intense, often painful or disgusted physical reaction to certain sensory experiences, individuals with AS have emotional difficulties related to their sensory processing. For example, they may become upset or anxious when students brush up against them in the hall because the touch is uncomfortable or painful. Most neurotypicals are able to modulate, or regulate, their reaction to sensory messages by ignoring some and paying attention to others. However, the modulation problems of many individuals with AS make their reaction to sensory input unpredictable. When children have poor modulation, their responses can vary quite dramatically from one situation to another, from very unresponsive to overly sensitive (Dunn et al., in press).

When Ben walked in the hallway between first and second hour, he was able to ignore that others were brushing up against him as they went by. However, by sixth hour, when someone crowded him, Ben flew into a rage and started yelling at the student about being insensitive and inconsiderate. This difference in reaction may be attributed to the level of anxiety experienced before the event or may have occurred because he had already had as much uncontrolled physical contact as he could tolerate that day.

What sensory problems exist in middle and high school? Consider the very middle and high school situations that most young people look forward to. They are filled with potential sensory problems. Take, for example, the cafeteria. Eating in the cafeteria is an overwhelming experience for many students with AS – the noise (auditory); the food (olfactory, gustatory); students bumping into each other (tactile); problems balancing the lunchtray, milk carton, silverware, and lunch money (vestibular; proprioception). In one 30-minute period, all of the adolescent's sensory systems can be overloaded. The result is a tantrum, rage, meltdown or shutdown.

The sensory systems can be bombarded in a variety of other situations. Walking through the halls during passing time offers many of the same sensory challenges seen in the lunchroom. Experiences during physical education class and the locker room can also assault the senses.

Behavior

Not all adolescents with AS have behavior problems. Those who do often are reacting to a world they see as unpredictable, unforgiving, and cruel. Considering the pressures listed below, it is no wonder the student with AS may experience a tantrum, rage, or meltdown:

- failure to understand rules and routines
- desire for friendships coupled with few skills to fulfill this wish
- disruptions from pursuing an all-encompassing special interest
- stress related to coping with the everyday challenges of change and overwhelming sensory input
- inability to protect oneself from teasing and bullying

Anxiety and Stress

High levels of stress and anxiety are prevalent among teens with AS for the reasons we have discussed previously. But the way teens with AS show stress can be deceiving. Therefore, it is important that others around them – parents, siblings, teachers, peers – know what signs to look for. Unlike many normally developing and achieving peers, teens with Asperger Syndrome may not reveal their stress through voice tone, body posture, and so forth. Because their cues are so subtle, their agitation often escalates to a point of crisis before others become aware of their discomfort.

Al, a middle school student with AS who is enrolled in advanced content courses, is academically capable of completing most of his work. However, his teachers expressed concerns about what they termed Al's "unpredictable tantrums." They were ready and prepared to prompt him to home base (discussed in Chapter 4), when necessary, but most of the time they were unable to detect the signs leading up to an approaching tantrum. One of Al's teachers, Mr. Moore, said that it appeared as if Al's meltdowns came from nowhere. As a result, the teachers were surprised to hear from Al's mother that he had a definite stress signal. When he ran his hand through his hair, it meant that he had "had enough." Recognizing this small cue helped Al's teachers to prompt him to home base, thereby preventing the occurrence of meltdowns. A program was also put in place to help Al recognize his own behavioral signal so that he could monitor his stress level himself.

Depression

Considering the alarming reports of anxiety and stress among adolescents with AS, it is not surprising to find a widespread prevalence of depression among these youth. Indeed, it is at this time in life that diagnosable depression often first occurs (Wing, 1981). In a recent study, 70% of the participants with AS were taking antidepressant medications (Barnhill, 2000). Anecdotal reports have also expressed alarm about the high number of individuals with AS who have been diagnosed with depression. In an attempt to determine the reasons why this disorder is so prevalent among adolescents with AS, Wing (1981) posited that depression may result from students with AS becoming aware that they are different from their peers. More specifically, Barnhill and Myles (in press) have suggested that depression in teens with AS may be related to how they perceive their successes and failures. A study of 33 adolescents with AS found that they tended to blame themselves if something negative occurred even if they logically could not have been at fault. Moreover, these teens felt that if they were to become involved in a similar situation again, this, too, would be doomed for failure.

> . . . anecdotal reports have also expressed alarm about the high number of individuals with AS who have been diagnosed with depression.

Ken was invited to a party at the home of one of his friends. He looked forward the party but was apprehensive about what he was supposed to do at the party. To help alleviate his anxiety, Ken and his parents carefully rehearsed what he could say and do in various situations likely to come up at the party. They practiced dancing and asking girls to dance. All went well, but on the night of the party, Ken accidentally spilled a drink down the front of his shirt right after he arrived. He was so mortified that he called his parents to pick him up immediately. Ken berated himself all the way home for being clumsy and never knowing how to do the right thing. Worse than that, the next time he received an invitation to a party, he turned it down because he "knew" that he would just spill something again and ruin everything.

Distractibility and Inattention

Attention deficit hyperactivity disorder (ADHD) is a label that many students with AS have previously been given. Teens with AS are often distracted by their environment. Instead of paying attention to the social studies lecture on Egypt, Tim attends to how the hair moves back and forth on the girl sitting in front of him. He is also distracted when he hears the word "Nefertiti." He immediately thinks of the black and white movie he saw the day before on the same topic and proceeds to rerun the script in his mind.

This type of distractibility is often referred to as daydreaming. During such times, the student looks as if he is paying attention, but he is not. As a result, teacher directions are not processed; student conversations are not heard (Myles & Southwick, 1999); and so on. Often the cause for such inattention is unknown, but it may be related to stress, a focus on an obsessive interest, or overstimulation.

External and Internal Tantrums, Rage, and Meltdowns

Not all students with AS have tantrums, rage, and meltdowns. However, the number who do is significant. These behavioral episodes have many causes. In adolescents, in particular, they range from not having a predictable daily schedule in school to fear of failure or embarrassment at not doing well academically.

The social environment also promotes tantrums, rage, and meltdowns. Adolescents with AS who desperately want to fit in with peers but are not able to do so often withdraw or express outward negative responses. This may include refusing to work with certain students, calling a teen who has bullied them a nasty name, or isolating themselves. Maria, an adolescent with AS, was made fun of by some students sitting near her in the cafeteria. To protect herself from teasing, she moved to another table and sat by herself. Michael was very concerned about his appearance and wanted to make sure he looked like everyone else. When a teen made fun of his shoes, he had a meltdown.

Sometimes stress that occurs at school releases itself at home. Thus, many parents report that their teens are too stressed out to complete homework at night because they need the after-school hours to calm down and relax.

Motor Skills

Fine- and gross-motor skills are a deficit in many adolescents with AS. Because of fine-motor problems, they cannot reflect their often high level of knowledge of a given subject in a handwritten report or complete an essay test, for example. Similar difficulties may be apparent in shop and industrial design classes where accuracy and small-motor movements are critial. Dressing out for physical education class is often a challenge for individuals with AS because of their fine-motor problems. For example, Lesley is late for gym every day because it takes her twice a long as her peers to change her clothes.

Gross-motor skills impact general appearance and may also inhibit participation in physical activities such as gym. Many students with AS are often characterized as clumsy or klutzy. As a result, they are often the last to be selected for team sports.

Visual-motor skills also affect school functioning. Victor, a high school student with AS, knows that he must watch the chair carefully as he sits down. Unlike his typical peers, he can't just sense where it is. He has learned this after falling off his chair numerous times and being laughed at by the other students or reprimanded by the teacher. Copying assignments from the board in school is also problematic. It is difficult for students with AS to look from the board to their paper and accurately copy the assignment in a timely fashion.

Summary

The characteristics of AS discussed in this chapter appear to be exacerbated by the complexity of the middle and high school environment. Many parents report that problems with their child that were manageable in elementary school become significant at the middle and high school levels. Puberty, coupled with a more complex school schedule and teacher expectations for increased student responsibility and higher academic performance, results in students with AS failing school even if they know the content. In addition, behavioral issues are more pronounced; emotionality is enhanced with frequent sudden mood swings.

Thrown into this mix is the often uncomfortable awareness of the opposite sex. Individuals with AS who have difficulty understanding their own feelings find it even more confusing when they "like someone."

The social stakes are higher when puberty sets in. As do all teenagers, individuals with AS want their parents to recede into the background. Yet, this is often impossible because although physical maturity may be evident, emotional maturity is not keeping pace. In fact, adolescents with AS often require more supervision at this age because misinterpretations of social cues can be devastating. When Jeff decided that he liked Ivy, he sent her a dozen roses. In his mind, that was all that was needed from the boyfriend-girlfriend relationship. His hourly calls to her are not returned, but Jeff still thinks of Ivy as his girlfriend.

The complex academic, behavioral, and social demands of adolescence present challenges to many neurotypical students, ranging from juggling after-school activities to completing homework, negotiating the hallways during passing, and maintaining a certain social sophistication. When adolescents with AS experience similar challenges, they are magnified because of the characteristics inherent in this exceptionality. Add the onset of puberty to the mix, and often these adolescents end up suffering from serious anxiety and depression with few of the skills needed to cope with their surroundings.

A high level of support and structure is needed so that students with AS can survive these tumultuous years. In the following chapters we offer suggestions for how to incorporate support and accommodations into the lives of youth with AS as a means of helping them become better adjusted, productive adults.

Chapter 3

Assessment of Adolescents with Asperger Syndrome

Because of the complexities of the middle and high school environment and the multifaceted needs of adolescents with AS, it is important that the educators who work with them have a comprehensive understanding of their social, behavioral, and academic needs. In an effort to provide the most appropriate and effective programming, assessment must include the following: (a) diagnostic assessment (if it has not previously been completed); (b) curriculum-based assessment of academic strengths and concerns; (c) formal and informal measures of sensory, social, and language skills; and (d) functional assessment of behaviors and perceptions.

Diagnostic Assessment

In most states, obtaining a diagnosis of Asperger Syndrome requires medical assistance. Physicians most often use the *Diagnostic and Statistical Manual-Fourth Edition Text Revision* (DSM-IV TR; American Psychiatric Association, 2000) or the *International Classification of Diseases and Related Health Problems* (ICD-10; World Health Organization, 1992). According to these documents, to receive a diagnosis of AS, an individual must demonstrate a social impairment but cannot exhibit a delay in language or cognitive development. In addition, he or she must exhibit patterns that can be described as restricted, repetitive, and/or stereotypic in behavior, interests, and activities.

However, it is difficult for medical professionals (or any other professionals, for that matter) to quickly and accurately ascertain the profile of a youth they are asked to diagnose. Brief observations are most often not sufficient to render a diagnosis. Thus, the medical community must rely on the observations and reports of those who know the individual best – parents and teachers. Faced with a myriad other day-to-day responsibilities, assembling this information can be cumbersome and time-consuming.

The *Asperger Syndrome Diagnostic Scale* (ASDS; Myles, Bock, & Simpson, 2000) can aid in diagnosis and make an otherwise daunting task less so. This 50-item instrument, which was normed on persons with AS, can be completed in approximately 15 minutes by individuals who know the person being diagnosed well. The ASDS items cover five areas: (a) language, (b) social, (c) maladaptions, (d) cognition, and (e) sensory-motor. For example, items in the social subscale ask raters whether the individual has difficulty (a) with the concept of personal space, (b) making and keeping friends despite a desire to do so, and (c) understanding the feelings of others. Respondents note the presence or absence of characteristics in each of these areas; the resulting score indicates the probability of the youth having AS. Parents or teachers can complete the ASDS and present it to the diagnostic professional, who can then use it as an aid in rendering a correct diagnosis.

Assessment of Physical Characteristics

It is important to rule out any medically based problems that could contribute to the student's social and academic problems. For example, school records should be reviewed to determine if recent hearing and vision screenings have been conducted. Other areas in the physical domain that merit consideration include the student's (a) physical size (small, average, large); (b) handedness (right, left, ambidextrous); (c) gross-motor skills (unusual gait, awkward, clumsy, jerky movements); (d) voice prosody (inflection, intonation); (e) fluency (stutters, pauses, difficulty retrieving words); (f) relevance of speech; (g) sensitivity to sensory stimuli (sound, light); (h) fatigue and sleep patterns; (i) appetite; (j) increased irritability or mood swings; and (k) increased withdrawal or loss of interest in previously enjoyed activities. Medications and their side effects should also be reviewed.

Curriculum-Based Assessment

Following an analysis of physical characteristics, it is important to determine the skills the student has as well as those he needs. Most school districts use norm-referenced standardized tests to assist in determining eligibility for special services. While many of these instruments report a high reliability and validity, they sometimes do not assess the skills with which individuals with AS have difficulty, nor do they translate into academic, behavioral, or social objectives.

Reading

For example, a reading test that identifies reading level through a combination of (a) number of words read correctly and (b) number of factual questions answered correctly does not accurately predict the reading level of a student with AS who faces other difficulties. These may include (a) making inferences, (b) predicting outcomes, (c) understanding characters' motivation and intention in stories, (d) differentiating relevant from irrelevant details, (e) naming the main idea, (f) drawing conclusions, (g) vocabulary (note: the distinction must be made between definitions the student has memorized and can repeat and those she actually understands), (h) sequencing, and (i) recall of story events without prompts or additional processing time.

In addition, the individual's reading problems may change by subject matter, classroom setting (whole group vs. individual setting), and stress level. Diagnosticians must ensure that reading decoding (traditionally a strength for students with AS) is not confused with reading comprehension (often a challenge). Thus, we recommend assessing these areas using the curriculum the student will be learning.

Writing

Generally, students with AS have difficulty (a) organizing their thoughts into a coherent sequence, (b) providing sufficient background and description to ensure reader understanding, and (c) creativity. For these reasons, written language assessment of students with AS should include these skills using both written and oral language samples with and without opportunities for brainstorming prior to writing.

As fine-motor problems make the physical task of writing difficult for many students with AS, writing mechanics can also be problematic. For example, students with AS may have trouble with letter formation, spacing, staying on the line, running out of space on the page, spelling, capitalization, punctuation, and grammar. Thus, handwritten and computer-generated stories should be compared as should near- and far-point copying to make sure a complete picture of the student's skills has been captured.

Social/Life Skills

At the middle and high school levels, the heavy academic emphasis in school often precludes teaching social skills or life skills. In response to teachers' question, "When is there time to teach social skills?," often the answer lies in making efficient use of time otherwise scheduled for academics.

A curriculum-based measure administered in each of the competency areas can indicate which information the student knows. If the student already knows the required information, why spend valuable time reteaching it? Instead, this time could be used to focus on social or life skills and enrichment (see Chapter 4), as appropriate.

Competency Testing

In a recent push to increase the performance of the nation's students, most states have developed a set of competencies in all major subject areas that students must master prior to graduation. These competencies and the way they are measured are usually contained in manuals that are available from counselors or administrators within the middle and high school. Teachers and parents should work together to administer a curriculum-based assessment in each of the areas covered in these manuals to determine which content the student knows and which content she does not know and thereby help prepare the student for the competency tests.

Margaret, a 12-year-old girl with AS, had special interests in history and geography. Just prior to her entering middle school, Margaret's social studies teacher, Mr. Malen, orally administered a curriculum-based assessment in social studies. He found that Margaret knew all the content at the sixth, seventh, and eighth grade levels. When the school team and Margaret's parents met about her IEP, they all agreed that Margaret did not need to complete the traditional middle school social studies track. Instead, they decided to devote a portion of the allocated social studies time to social skills instruction with the remainder of the time devoted to social studies geared toward Margaret's individual needs. Specifically, the social studies curriculum for Margaret included an area that had been targeted as a concern for her – completion of long-term projects.

Special considerations must be made for students with AS who most likely will attend college.

Margaret's social studies curriculum contained two components: (a) enriched materials from the middle school social studies curriculum and (b) materials from high school social studies-related coursework. Her assignments would be projects to be completed over time. For each project, Margaret would focus on (a) developing a timeline to complete the project, (b) budgeting time each evening for the project, (c) keeping herself on track, and (d) organizing the project. Mr. Malen astutely pointed out that before giving her content from the high school curriculum, he would like to administer a sophomore curriculum-based measure on social studies-related content to Margaret. This was a wise move since further assessment revealed that Margaret was ready to learn content typically provided to high school seniors.

Planning for College

In addition, special considerations must be made for students with AS who most likely will attend college. Although it is difficult to predict at this stage which college the youth may attend, some general considerations of college attendance can be made. For example, examining the liberal arts requirements of a local community college is a valuable starting point. In this way, educators working with the college-bound student with AS can ensure that the high school curriculum provides the appropriate prerequisites.

Measures of Sensory–Motor, Social, Language, and Student Learning Traits

Because youth with AS often experience sensory, social, and language challenges, it is important that each of these areas be carefully assessed. A variety of formal and informal measures may be used for this purpose. Formal assessments include norm-referenced and standardized instruments that provide a comparison of a student's performance to the profiles of typically developing peers. Informal assessments, which consist of inventories/checklists, parent and student interviews, and direct observations, offer descriptive information that can be used to create goals and objectives.

The degree of challenge a student demonstrates and the type of information needed to develop an effective educational program typically dictate the kinds of assessment that are used. In most cases, parent and student interviews yield important information that can be translated directly to programming. In the following discussion only a few instruments are highlighted for each of the major challenging areas for students with AS. Many others exist that can provide similar information. Discussion of a particular assessment measure does not mean that we view it as the best and/or the only measure; it merely serves as an example.

Sensory-Motor Skills

Individuals with AS can be hyper- and/or hyposensitive to sensory stimuli in the tactile, vestibular, proprioception, visual, auditory, gustatory, and olfactory areas (see Table 2.1). These sensory sensitivities may not be evident from a brief or cursory observation of the student's behavior. To further complicate matters, these sensitivities tend to fluctuate depending on a variety of variables such as the activity involved, the individual's emotional state at the time, as well as environmental demands.

A variety of formal and informal instruments provide information about sensory processing. Most of them require the special skills of an occupational therapist to be administered and interpreted appropriately (Myles et al., 2000). *The Sensory Profile* (Dunn, 1999), the *Short Sensory Profile* (McIntosh, Miller, Shyu, & Dunn, 1999), *Sensory Integration Inventory-Revised* (Reisman & Hanschu,

1992); *Adolescent/Adult Checklist for Occupational Therapy* (Occupational Therapy Associates Watertown, 1997); *Sensory Screening* (Yak, Sutton, & Aquilla, 1998); and *Questions to Guide Classroom Observations* (Kientz & Miller, 1999) are all instruments that can assess sensory-related skills. (For a description of each, refer to Myles et al., 2000.)

Social Skills

Good social skills are important at every stage of our lives, but nowhere do they play a more critical role than during adolescence. This is particularly true for youths with AS. Most adolescents with AS want to have friends and interact with others just like their typical peers. To be successful in this area, they need to understand how to get along with others on a one-to-one basis, how to act in a group, how to recognize teasing and sarcasm, how to get along with teachers, and so on.

Unfortunately for many youths with AS, adolescence is a painful time – filled with teasing and ridicule. Johnny, a fifth grader with AS in a general education class, is allowed to go to the library to read every morning as soon as his bus arrives. Prior to that arrangement, Johnny was the frequent target of teasing during the unstructured time before students were allowed into the school building because of his awkward social interactions.

Interactional demands become more complex as we get older. It is therefore important to assess social interactions that occur on a variety of levels. Areas of social interaction that require assessment include (a) with adults, (b) with familiar peers the student likes, (c) with familiar peers the student does not like, (d) with peers who like the student with AS, (e) with unfamiliar peers, (f) in structured settings, and (g) in unstructured settings.

A systematic assessment of social skills is particularly important because many youth with AS demonstrate splinter skills – they have learned some higher-level skills by rote but do not have the lower-level skills to make these skills meaningful. For example, Jon knows how to lead a group activity, but does not have some of the prerequisite skills for being a successful leader, such as sharing materials and taking turns spontaneously.

Several informal scope-and-sequence charts can be used to assess the social interaction skills of persons with AS. These include (a) *Skillstreaming the Adolescent – Revised* (Goldstein, 1997); (b) *Developmental Therapy Objectives Rating Form – Revised* (from *Developmental Therapy-Developmental Teaching*, 3rd ed.; Wood, Davis, Swindle, & Quirk, 1996); (c) *Diagnostic Analysis of Nonverbal Accuracy* (DANVA; Nowicki, 1997); (d) *The Walker Social Skills Curriculum: The ACCEPTS Program* (Walker, McConnell, Holmes, Todis, Walker, & Golden, 1988); and (e) *Connecting with Others: Lessons for Teaching Social and Emotional Competence* (Richardson, 1996).

Answers to the following questions supplement the information gleaned from some of the instruments listed above to arrive at a clearer picture of the student's social skills and social life, thereby helping educators better understand the social skills and challenges of the youth with AS.

1. How much supervision and what types of adaptations has the student required for successful interaction with adults? With peers?
2. What types of social difficulties has the student experienced in unstructured situations and what supports and accommodations were necessary to minimize these problems?
3. Is this student perceived by peers as "obviously" different?
4. Is there a need for peer awareness training?
5. Is there a type of peer group in which this student's differences are markedly less noticeable? More noticeable?
6. What instances of teasing/bullying have occurred within the school environment? Did they occur primarily with one or two individual students or with several groups of students? What was successful in reducing these instances? How did the student with AS respond to teasing/bullying?
7. Who are the peers who like/tolerate the student with AS?
8. Is it difficult to get peers to work with the student?
9. Does the student with AS like certain students? Are the feelings mutual?
10. What teachers/administrators have worked particularly well with this student? Why?
11. Have any school personnel had significant difficulty with the

student with AS? What factors seem to have been the major problem in these instances?

Language

Language assessments that exclusively or primarily test knowledge of grammar, vocabulary, and sentence structure typically reveal that adolescents with AS are functioning in the average to above-average range. But it is important not to stop there. People who work with individuals with AS recognize language difficulties that center around pragmatics – the social part of language. For example, individuals with AS have difficulty interpreting literal language such as metaphors, idioms, or words used sarcastically; problem solving; and communicative intent.

To access skills related to communicative intent, Sally Bligh (cited in Michael Thompson Productions, 2000) suggests looking at how the student uses language. Specifically, she asks, (a) Is he using language just to convey information? or (b) Is he using information to establish social relationships with adults? Usually the latter is an area of weakness, while the former is often a strength.

Prosody, the melody or intonation of the voice, should also be assessed as some individuals with AS have an unusual voice tone. Finally, issues related to the following areas should be investigated: (a) ability to change topics, (b) talking with rather than talking at people, (c) vocabulary complexity, and (d) establishing mutual attention.

Direct observation of interactions between the individual with AS and neurotypical peers is essential to determine the communication skills the student uses spontaneously. Interactions with peers are typically of a different nature than those occurring with adults. That is, adults often follow the individual's lead in conversation, wait for a response, tolerate lengthy monologues, and find pedantic phrasing interesting. Peers, on the other hand, don't support these conversational idiosyncrasies, and it is in these interactions that the individual with AS has most trouble. Problems in language have devastating results and must be pursued. Table 3.1 lists a sample of language tests that tap areas in which persons with AS are particularly challenged.

TABLE 3.1
Language Tests

Title, Author, Publisher	Year	Administration Time	Age Range	Subtests	Assessment Instrument Review
Clinical Evaluation of Language Fundamentals – Third Edition Semel, Wiig, & Secord The Psychology Corporation	1995	30-45 min	6-21:11	Sentence Structure; Word Structure; Concepts & Directions; Formulated Sentences; Word Classes; Recalling Sentences; Sentence Assembly; Semantic Relationships; Supplementary subtests: Word Associations; Listening to Paragraphs; Rapid, Automatic Naming	Stimuli/Components/Scoring: excellent Standardization: excellent Purpose/Product/Match: excellent
Comprehensive Receptive and Expressive Vocabulary Test Wallace & Hammill Pro-Ed, Inc.	1994	20-30 min	4-17:11	Receptive Vocabulary, Expressive Vocabulary	Stimuli/Components/Scoring: good Standardization: excellent Purpose/Product/Match: good
Peabody Picture Vocabulary Test – Revised Dunn & Dunn American Guidance Service	1981	10-15 min	2:6-40:11	NA	Stimuli/Components/Scoring: good Standardization: good Purpose/Product/Match: good

TABLE 3.1 *(continued)*
Language Tests

Title, Author, Publisher	Year	Administration Time	Age Range	Subtests	Assessment Instrument Review
Test of Language Competence-Expanded Edition (Level 2) Wiig & Secord The Psychology Corporation	1989	1 hour	9-18:11	Ambiguous Sentences, Making Inferences, Recreating Sentences, Understanding Metaphoric Expressions	Stimuli/Components/Scoring: good Standardization: excellent Purpose/Product/Match: good
Test of Pragmatic Language Phelps-Tarasaki & Phelps-Gunn Pro-Ed, Inc.	1992	45 min	5-13:11	NA	Stimuli/Components/Scoring: good Standardization: good Purpose/Product/Match: limited
Test of Problem Solving-Adolescent Zachman, Barrett, Huisingh, Orman, & Blagden LinguiSystems	1994	40 min	12-17:11	NA	Stimuli/Components/Scoring: excellent Standardization: excellent Purpose/Product/Match: good

Source: Harris, L. G., & Shelton, I. S. (1996). *Desk reference of assessment instruments in speech and language.* San Antonio, TX: Communication Skill Builders. *Compiled by Stephanie D. Stansberry.*

Student Learning Traits [2]

Student learning traits provide "insight into the manner in which facts, information, and concepts are acquired and used" (Myles, Constant, Simpson, & Carlson, 1989, p. 11). For assessment purposes, student learning traits can be grouped into five categories: (a) learning style, (b) behavioral patterns, (c) strategies (Myles et al., 1989), (d) environmental predictability, and (e) behavior/emotional regulation. Knowledge about student learning traits assists in determining the types of accommodations and special supports needed to facilitate school success.

Learning style

Learning style refers to the way a person approaches a task and learns information from the environment. It includes (a) long- and short-term memory; (b) part-to-whole versus whole-to-part learning; (c) incidental learning; (d) work habits; and (e) generalization. Insight gained from assessing learning styles can be used to determine how instruction should be approached for the student with AS (Myles et al., 1989). Specific questions that can guide observations of learning style appear in Table 3.2.

Behavioral patterns

Observations of interpersonal skills, stressors, eye contact as well as on- and off-task behaviors are of particular importance when assessing individuals with AS. Other behavioral traits that impact learning and socialization include impulsivity/compulsivity, distractibility, excessive movement, attention-seeking, and avoidance behaviors (Myles et al., 1989).

Strategies

The third area of student learning traits, strategies, refers to the rules or techniques the student uses to manipulate, store, and retrieve information. The term is used broadly to refer to any techniques that lead to a response to an academic task or social situation.

---

[2] Authored with contributions from Jennifer Stella, University of Colorado Health Sciences Center; Joyce Anderson Downing, Central Missouri State University; and Judith K. Carlson, University of Missouri – Kansas City.

Table 3.2
Student Learning Traits Assessment

LEARNING STYLE

Long- and Short-Term Memory

1. Does student demonstrate both long- and short-term memory across all academic and social areas?
2. Does the quality and quantity of information in long-term memory differ if the student is presented with the information verbally versus in written form?
3. How does the student memorize information that she needs to learn?

Rote vs. Meaningful Memory

4. Does the student tend to learn rote easier than meaningful information?
5. Does the student learn information better if he hears it or sees it?
6. Does the student perform or complete a routine, but confuse or miss specific steps?

Part-to-Whole vs. Whole-to-Part Learning

7. Does the student begin a new task by scanning the material to gain some insight into the content or does he attend to every detail?
8. Does the student learn better using a part-to-whole or whole-to-part format? In math, whole-to-part learners learn the concept first and then the facts. These are the learners who have to know why or how something works before they can focus on memorization. Part-to-whole learners use the reverse strategy, memorizing facts without necessarily understanding their basis.

Incidental Learning

9. When does incidental learning occur? Is it seen in academic or social areas?
10. What conditions or environments must exist for incidental learning to occur?
11. What type of teacher or peer actions does the student imitate without instruction?

Work Habits

12. Does the student arrive in class on time?
13. How does the teacher give directions and instruction to the class (i.e., oral, written demonstration)?
14. If the teacher uses different methods of giving instructions, does the student respond better to a particular type of instruction and if so which (i.e., oral, written, demonstration, other)?
15. Does the student follow lecture content by answering questions when called upon or volunteering to answer questions?
16. Does the student attempt to add information to the discussion? Is this information relevant to the discussion? overly detailed?
17. Does the student continually ask for repetition of directions? If so, how often in a 20-minute period?

Table 3.2 *(continued)*
Student Learning Traits Assessment

18. Can the student turn to the correct page in a textbook when instructed to do so?
19. Does the student start tasks without prompting?
20. Does the student tend to start tasks right away or does he need time to acclimate to begin working?
21. What does the student do if he does not know how to start or complete a task?
22. Does the student require written, oral or pictorial instructions to begin, maintain or complete a task? How many directions can the student follow in each mode?
23. Are specific words (such as "wh" words) in assignments associated with task completion or noncompletion?
24. Does the student tend to rush through tasks or complete each problem systematically? Does this style differ across academic subjects?
25. Under what circumstances does the student complete work independently?
26. Does the student need to complete one task before beginning another?
27. How long can the student remain on task? Does on-task behavior differ by subject, type of presentation or medium used? How is off-task behavior demonstrated? What decreases off-task behavior?
28. In what situations does off-task behavior occur (seatwork, silent reading, lecture/discussion, cooperative learning)?
29. When presented with a task beyond the independent or instructional level, what behaviors does the student demonstrate (daydreaming, fidgeting, playing with objects, playing with clothing, making noises, making faces, leaving seat, talking to peers, calling out)? What specific tasks induce this behavior? How does the environment reinforce the response to stress?
30. How does the student request help for a task?
31. Does the student require continuous encouragement from the teacher to stay on task?
32. How does the student's rate of production compare with peers (fast, appropriate, slow)?
33. Which tasks does the student approach with enthusiasm?

Generalization

34. What type of information does the student generalize across settings, people, tasks, and time?
35. How did the student learn this information?

BEHAVIORAL PATTERNS

Peer/Group Interactions

1. Does the student actively interact with others or engage in parallel activities near others?
2. Does the student initiate interactions with others? How is this accomplished?

Table 3.2 *(continued)*
Student Learning Traits Assessment

3. Does the student consistently interact with one peer or engage in multiple interactions?
4. How closely does the student sit to peers and adults?

Response to Reinforcement

5. Is the student's performance enhanced by a reinforcement system? If so, what type and how often is reinforcement is used? When does satiation occur?
6. Does the student seek adult appreciation for task completion?
7. Does the student respond primarily to reinforcement or task completion?

Eye Contact

8. How often does the student initiate eye contact?
9. Does the student respond to teacher directions by looking up when the teacher begins to speak?
10. What methods, if any, does the teacher use to get the student's attention (i.e., teacher calls student's name, teacher physically approaches student, peers prompt student)?
11. How does the student respond to prompts for eye contact?
12. What behaviors accompany eye contact?

Sense of Humor

13. Does the student demonstrate a sense of humor?
14. How is it demonstrated?
15. What prompts expressions of humor?
16. Does the student tell jokes that make sense?
17. How does the student share his sense of humor?
18. How does the student respond to others' jokes?

Self-Stimulatory Behaviors

19. What self-stimulatory behaviors does the student exhibit?
20. When do the behaviors occur?
21. What is the communicative intent of the behaviors?
22. What type of redirection is used to stop self-stimulatory behaviors?

Perseveration

23. Does the student exhibit oral, motor or written perseveration?
24. What prompts such behavior?
25. How is this behavior stopped?

Impulsive/Compulsive Behaviors

26. What type of impulsive/compulsive behaviors does the student engage in?
27. When are they most likely to be occur?
28. Are they associated with frustration, communication problems, fear or lack of structure?

Table 3.2 *(continued)*
Student Learning Traits Assessment

Distractibility

29. How does the student exhibit distractibility?
30. Is type of task associated with distractibility?
31. Is the student distracted by auditory or visual stimuli?
32. How is the student redirected to task?

Excessive Movement

33. When does the student exhibit excessive movement?
34. What are the characteristics of this movement?
35. Does the student redirect self or is teacher redirection required? Describe how redirection occurs.
36. Is excessive movement associated with any particular situation, environment, task, or person?

Avoidance Behaviors

37. What tasks does the student consider undesirable?
38. What behaviors does the student exhibit during those tasks?
39. How do teachers respond to the student's avoidance behaviors?

Attention-Seeking Behaviors

40. What attention-seeking behaviors does the student exhibit toward adults? students?
41. When are these behaviors likely to occur?
42. How do teachers (peers) respond to these behaviors?

STRATEGIES

Strategic Learning

1. What self-developed strategies does the student use? When are they used?
2. Are these strategies effective in more than one situation?
3. Does the student monitor the accuracy or success of the strategy?
4. Are self-stimulatory behaviors substitutes for inefficient strategies?

Learning/Memory Strategies

5. Does the student learn and apply teacher-instructed strategies without prompts?
6. How many trials are required for mastery?
7. Does the student require direct instruction to facilitate generalization?

Self-Verbalization

8. Does the student use self-verbalization (talking oneself through a task) to learn or complete tasks?
9. When is self-verbalization seen?
10. Does self-verbalization aid in task completion or does it operate merely as a self-stimulatory behavior?

Table 3.2 *(continued)*
Student Learning Traits Assessment

Self-Correction

11. Does the student self-monitor work for errors?
12. Does the student correct errors with teacher assistance?
13. Is the student so overly concerned about correctness that it interferes with task completion?

Organizational Skills

14. Does the student demonstrate "internal" organizational skills?
15. Do these skill enhance or inhibit task completion?
16. Is organization centered around time, place, space or individuals?
17. Are organizational skills generalized?
18. Describe the organization of the student's backpack and locker.
19. Can the student find the necessary materials when needed?

Problem-Solving Strategies

20. How does the student react to an unknown situation?
21. How readily can the student learn and apply a problem-solving strategy to an academic situation? social situation?
22. What motivates the student to apply a problem-solving strategy versus leaving a problem unsolved?

ENVIRONMENTAL PREDICTABILITY

1. Does the student participate in "specials" (art, music, physical education, etc.)? If not, why?
2. Does the student exhibit an overreliance on routines?
3. How does the student respond to an unannounced change in structure such as the following: (a) physical structure changes in the classroom, (b) seating changes, (c) time changes, (d) changes in location of activity, (e) changes in order of events, (f) addition to/deletion from routine, (g) cancellation of activity, (h) teacher absence or (i) friend absence?
4. Do advance organizers or priming alter the student's behavior? If so, are the advance organizers or priming presented in oral or written format?
5. To what extent does the student require a warning of upcoming changes in routine or schedule for the following: (a) physical structure changes in the classroom, (b) seating changes, (c) time changes, (d) activity location changes, (e) order of events changes, (f) addition to/deletion from routine (g) cancellation of an activity, (h) teacher absent or (i) friend absent?
6. How does the student perform when he has a substitute teacher?

Table 3.2 *(continued)*
Student Learning Traits Assessment

EMOTIONAL/BEHAVIORAL REGULATION

1. What is the student's behavioral state when working independently on seatwork? silent reading? discussion/lecture? cooperative group experiences (i.e., interested, confused, distracted, anxious, bored, calm)?
2. What emotions does the student recognize in himself?
3. For each of these emotions, does the student understand the variable that may elicit the emotion?
4. How does the student exhibit mild frustration? severe frustration? mild concern? other emotions?
5. Does the student know when she needs to use home base?
   If so, what is the indicator?
6. Does the student seek out home base or a safe person on her own?
7. Does the student respond to teacher prompts for home base? What type of assistance is needed?
8. What behaviors signal the student's need for home base?
9. What does the student do to self-calm? How long does this process typically take?
10. In what situations is the student likely to "overreact"?
11. What behaviors typify her overreaction?
12. Does the student respect authority?
13. Has the student been considered destructive? Under what conditions did this behavior occur?

From *Asperger Syndrome and Assessment: Practical Solutions for Identifying Students' Needs,* by B. S. Myles, D. Adreon, & J. Stella, in press. Shawnee Mission, KS: AAPC. Reprinted with permission.

Strategies include (a) strategic learning skills, (b) learning/memory strategies, (c) self-verbalization, (d) self-correction, (e) organizational skills, and (f) problem solving (Myles et al., 1989).

Environmental predictability

An assessment of environmental predictability looks at the student's need for structure in academic and social situations. For example, responses to routines, unanticipated changes, and substitute teachers fall into this category. In addition, the type of supports needed to assist the student in being flexible is an important aspect of assessing environmental predictability.

Behavior/emotional regulation

Students with AS have problems regulating their behavior and emotions. For example, even under the most ideal conditions, many cannot communicate whether they feel content, mildly distressed, or anxious. This situation is exacerbated when the student experiences stressors that impede academic or socially functioning. In our clinical experience, the majority of students with Asperger Syndrome are not able to recognize their own emotional state when it has reached the point where school personnel might expect them to go to a safe person or home base (see Chapter 4). Thus, it is important to understand how the student perceives her emotions and controls them.

A thorough assessment of a student's learning traits can help the school team and parents plan a program that takes into account the student's strengths, concerns, idiosyncrasies, and understanding of the world around him. While it is important to assess the content a student knows, this provides only a snapshot at a particular point in time. Student learning traits, on the other hand, tend to be longer lasting and therefore provide insight into how instruction should occur in order to facilitate learning. The items addressed here are many and varied. Student learning traits are best assessed through direct observation as well as through teacher and parent interviews. In addition, students themselves can often provide insight into their own learning traits.

Functional Assessment of Behaviors and Perceptions

Functional assessment determines why a behavior or set of behaviors occur. The idea behind functional assessment is that once we understand the behavior, the environment, the student's perceptions and reactions, and peers' and adults' perceptions and reactions, we can plan an intervention that will be effective. Without a sound understanding of these factors, some interventions actually make behaviors worse (O'Neill et al., 1997).

Student behaviors do not occur in isolation, nor are they random. They are associated with a reason or cause. Thus, behaviors are a form of communication. Functional assessment is a first step in developing effective interventions based on such behavioral messages. Six steps make up a functional assessment:
1. identify and describe student behavior
2. describe setting demands and antecedents
3. collect baseline data and/or work samples
4. complete functional analysis measures and develop a hypothesis
5. develop and implement a behavioral intervention plan
6. collect data and follow up to analyze the effectiveness of the plan

Identify and Describe the Student's Behavior

Most basic to the process of functional assessment is identifying and describing the behavior around which an intervention is to be structured. When examining the student's behavior, it is important to clearly operationalize the behavior or behaviors that are evident. Behaviors are stated in observable terms so that everyone who comes in contact with the student recognizes the same behaviors. By contrast, if student behaviors are amorphously defined, chances are that not all educators will recognize them and, therefore, may not apply the designated interventions at the appropriate time.

A behavior identified as "the student shows stress," for example, does little to help the middle school team understand when the student with AS is about to have a meltdown. Behaviors must be described as verbs with information on how they are performed, how often they occur, how long they last, and how intense they are. For example, based on the observation "the student under stress begins to pace rapidly back and forth while whispering," the teacher can easily recognize the behavior.

Describe Setting Demands and Antecedents

When analyzing student behaviors, it is necessary to describe the environment both in situations where the student is experiencing problems and in classes where few or no problems occur. Comparing these two types of settings often yields a clue to behavior problems and their origins.

Niral's middle school team and parents were concerned about his frequent refusal to work and his subsequent shutdown (laying his head on his desk until the period ended) whenever an English literature quiz was given. Both the team and Niral's parents were sure that he understood the material he read and was completing the reading before the quiz was given. After some checking, they found that this behavior only occurred in English literature class. In probing further, they discovered that in all other classes tests were either multiple-choice or offered an option to be taken verbally, whereas the literature tests were usually in essay format. This one clue helped provide an answer to Niral's refusal behaviors.

As Niral's case illustrates, before designing an intervention, it is important to fully understand the environments in which the behavior is and is not likely to occur. To make this task easier and more effective, the Autism Asperger Syndrome Resource Center (1997) designed a checklist, Classroom Setting Demands (CSD). The CSD helps describe the classroom environment by asking specific questions regarding (a) teaching methods, (b) grading, (c) tests, (d) teaching materials, (e) product requirements, (f) student behavior, (g) class management, and (h) class structure. All of these components are integral to understanding why a behavior may be occurring. An adaptation of the CSD checklist appears in Figure 3.1. If each of the student's teachers completes a CSD or a similar form, a picture of the student's environments begins to emerge. Other factors related to setting demands include instructional expectations, behavioral expectations, and social demands.

Fourteen best practices for classroom instruction at the middle school level have been identified. These range from having a meaningful and functional curriculum to knowing the student's special health care needs (Kennedy & Fisher, 2001). A global assessment of the use of these 14 practices should be conducted in each of the student's classes. Table 3.3 provides a list and brief description of these 14 best practices for the classroom.

Collect Baseline Data and/or Work Samples

As mentioned, direct observations should be conducted both in environments where the targeted behavior occurs and where it does not occur. Observation data, an important component of the func-

Setting Demands

Name: _____ Class: _____ Date: _____

Circle the number that best answers each question or fill in the blank space provided.

TEACHING METHODS
A. % of class time spent in lecture . . . . . _____%
B. % of class time spent in discussion . . _____%
C. % of learning done through
    independent study . . . . _____%
D. % of time in cooperative
    learning groups . . . . _____%

	Never	Sometimes		Always
E. Is there a consistent daily routine? 1	2	3	4	5
F. Is there a consistent weekly routine?. 1	2	3	4	5

COMMENTS: _____

_____

GRADES	Never	Sometimes		Always
A. Is extra credit work accepted and/or encouraged? . 1	2	3	4	5
B. Can students rework previous assignments? 1	2	3	4	5
C. Is the grading criteria established and posted at				
the beginning of the course?. 1	2	3	4	5

COMMENTS: _____

_____

TESTS	Never	Sometimes		Always
A. Is a variety of test methods used in your class? . . . 1	2	3	4	5
1. Multiple-choice tests? 1	2	3	4	5
2. Essay tests? 1	2	3	4	5
3. Matching tests? 1	2	3	4	5
4. True/false tests? 1	2	3	4	5
5. Open-book tests? 1	2	3	4	5
6. Take-home tests? 1	2	3	4	5
7. Group/cooperative tests? 1	2	3	4	5
B. Are tests given in your class? 1	2	3	4	5
1. Daily tests?. 1	2	3	4	5
2. Weekly tests? 1	2	3	4	5
3. Monthly tests?. 1	2	3	4	5
4. Quarterly tests?. 1	2	3	4	5
C. Do you allow test-taking assistance? 1	2	3	4	5

COMMENTS: _____

_____

Figure 3.1. *Setting demands checklist.*

TEACHING MATERIALS Never Sometimes Always
A. Do you use a textbook? 1 2 3 4 5
B. Do you use handouts? 1 2 3 4 5
C. Do students need to bring outside materials to class? 1 2 3 4 5
   List materials needed: _____

D. Are prerequisite skills required? 1 2 3 4 5
   List skills: _____

E. Are typing/word processing skills required? 1 2 3 4 5
COMMENTS: _____

WRITTEN & OTHER MAJOR PRODUCTS Never Sometimes Always
A. Are students required to write in complete sentences? 1 2 3 4 5
B. Are students required to write paragraphs? 1 2 3 4 5
C. Are students required to write essays or
   3-5 paragraphs? 1 2 3 4 5
D. Is a research paper required? 1 2 3 4 5
E. Is an oral presentation required? 1 2 3 4 5
F. Are there any required major course
   projects/assignments? 1 2 3 4 5
   List: _____
G. How often do you require students to answer
   questions in written form? 1 2 3 4 5
COMMENTS: _____

STUDENT BEHAVIOR Never Sometimes Always
A. Is on-time behavior factored into the grade? 1 2 3 4 5
B. Is attendance factored into the grade? 1 2 3 4 5
C. Is student participation factored into the grade? . . . 1 2 3 4 5
D. Is work completion factored into the grade? 1 2 3 4 5
E. Are other student behaviors factored into the grade? 1 2 3 4 5
   List behaviors (i.e., on-task behavior, listening, etc.): _____

F. Is student notetaking an important part of your class? 1 2 3 4 5
G. Are students expected to manage their out-of-class
   behavior independently? 1 2 3 4 5
COMMENTS: _____

Figure 3.1. *(continued)*

BEHAVIOR MANAGEMENT   Never   Sometimes   Always

A. Does classroom staff use positive reinforcement to
   create a positive learning environment?. 1   2   3   4   5
B. Does teacher(s) respond to inappropriate
   behaviors in a consistent manner? 1   2   3   4   5
C. Are teacher responses to inappropriate behavior
   effective in reducing/stopping the behavior? 1   2   3   4   5
D. Do behavior management strategies include a
   focus on teaching appropriate behaviors rather
   than solely on punishment? 1   2   3   4   5
E. Does the student receive individualized reinforcement
   for appropriate behaviors, remaining on task,
   and completing assignments?. 1   2   3   4   5
F. Is the student prompted to leave the classroom
   when exhibiting inappropriate behaviors? 1   2   3   4   5
G. Is the student prompted to leave the classroom
   before behaviors become unmanageable?. 1   2   3   4   5

COMMENTS: _____

_____

CLASS MANAGEMENT   Never   Sometimes   Always

A. Are rules and guidelines posted and
   reviewed in your classroom?. 1   2   3   4   5
B. Are consequences clearly communicated
   to the students?. 1   2   3   4   5
C. Do you use material reinforcements? 1   2   3   4   5
D. Do you use other reinforcements?. 1   2   3   4   5
   List: _____

COMMENTS: _____

_____

CLASSROOM STRUCTURE

A. What is your present classroom seating arrangement?
   Draw a quick picture, circling where the target student is seated.

        Example   Your room

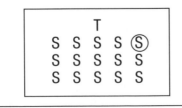

Figure 3.1. *(continued)*

B. What is the student's orientation to the blackboard
and teacher? (Is the student facing both or does
he have to move or twist to see?)
List: _____

C. Is the student seated away from distractions or
high-traffic areas? (such as near wastebasket,
pencil sharpener, door) 1   2   3   4   5

D. Is there an area in the classroom where the
student can go to minimize distractions
or calm himself? 1   2   3   4   5

E. Are the peers seated around the student
positive role models? 1   2   3   4   5

F. How often are students in the above
seating arrangements? 1   2   3   4   5

G. What other alternate arrangements do you use?
List: _____

H. How often are students in the above alternate
seating arrangements? 1   2   3   4   5

COMMENTS: _____
_____

Figure 3.1. *(continued)*

Note. Adapted from *Assessing the Setting Demands in the Classroom,* Autism Asperger
Syndrome Resource Center (www.KUMC.edu/AARC).

tional assessment process, are collected to document behavior frequency, duration, and/or intensity (Kerr & Nelson, 1993). The *Student Learning Traits Assessment* mentioned earlier can be used for this activity (see Table 3.2).

Whenever possible, permanent products or work samples should also be analyzed to determine student achievement rate across academic settings. Specifically, work samples should be analyzed for (a) quality or "neatness," (b) completion, (c) turn-in percentage, and (d) organization.

Table 3.3
Fourteen Best Practices for Classroom Instruction

Recommended Best Practice	Brief Description
Meaningful and functional curriculum	Is the material being taught to the student useful to him or her and relevant to his or her daily life? Providing a meaningful and functional curriculum is an important means of increasing student motivation to work with instructional materials.
Facilitating membership	Do students with and without disabilities have regular, daily opportunities to interact and develop relationships with each other? Frequent social interactions with other students allow for relationship development and improve students' social competence.
Providing choices	Are students allowed to actively choose the focus and content of instructional materials? This component is important because it increases students' interest in instructional materials and allows them to actively choose some of the content of their curriculum.
Varying instructional materials	Are the means by which instructional materials are presented to students varied from period to period and day to day? Actively varying the means by which students contact instructional materials improves their attention during instruction and their learning.
Implementing age-appropriate materials	Are the materials and content that are being taught to students something that their typically developing peers frequently use? This is important because it provides students with relevant instructional experiences that they can relate to their peers.

Table 3.3 *(continued)*

Fourteen Best Practices for Classroom Instruction

Recommended Best Practice	Brief Description
Attending to positive student behavior	Are students provided with attention from teachers primarily for engaging in appropriate and desirable behavior? The provision of teacher attention for appropriate behavior is important because it teaches students in which behaviors they should engage.
Predicting schedules	Is each student able to understand and predict in which activities he or she is being asked to engage? Making educational routines predictable allows students to understand why they are being asked to terminate an activity, what will be occurring next, and what they receive for participating.
Learning strategies for groups	Is a variety of group learning strategies used as a means for students to learn instructional material? Providing students with regular opportunities to learn to cooperate and interact with each other is an effective means of increasing learning.
Incorporating learning styles	Different students have different patterns of learning and engaging in instructional materials. Do teaching strategies accommodate for individual students? This is important to do, because it allows each student to receive maximum benefit from instruction.
Focusing on student	Do student interests and preferences provide the basis for instructional content? This is important because students are less likely to emit problem behavior when they are engaged in activities that they like to do.
Modeling appropriate behavior	Do teachers and peers actively model how students should behave for them to be more effective learners? Modeling is a very effective means of teaching students and allows them to see others engaging in successful and appropriate learning experiences.

Table 3.3 *(continued)*

Fourteen Best Practices for Classroom Instruction

Recommended Best Practice	Brief Description
Using student-based interdisciplinary teams	Are teachers and administrators using school-based teams to work collectively on improving the behavior of students? Working as a team provides a variety of perspectives, experiences, and skills to be brought together to solve problems and proactively plan.
Knowing medications	Are any students receiving medication that might affect their behavior? Teachers need to know what the primary effects, side effects, and long-term effects of a medication are so they can monitor its impact on student performance.
Knowing special health care needs	Do students have any identified or suspected special health care needs? Students should be monitored regularly for special health care needs and receive regular checkups from health personnel, especially prior to the development of a positive behavior support plan, to assess for the existence of possible health care issues relating to problem behavior.

From *Inclusive Middle Schools* (pp. 110–111), by C.H. Kennedy & D. Fisher, 2001. Baltimore: Paul H. Brookes Publishing Co. Used with permission.

Complete Functional Analysis Measures and Develop a Hypothesis

To most effectively and efficiently intervene with a problem behavior, it is important to understand the causes or functions of that behavior. The goal of functional assessment and related intervention procedures is not simply to eradicate a behavior but to help the student learn new and more appropriate ways of getting his needs met. Researchers and practitioners have developed a list of hypotheses for why problem behaviors occur. These appear in Table 3.4. Understanding what causes behavior is one of the initial steps in setting up an effective intervention.

Understanding the perspective of the individual with AS is also important for developing effective programming. The interview outlined in Figure 3.2 can aid in this process. Items are intended to elicit the student's likes and dislikes related to peers, teachers, and social and academic demands as well as to provide information on each of his classes.

Table 3.4
Possible Reasons Why Problem Behaviors Occur

Failure to understand or know what to do
Wish to escape or avoid certain tasks/situations
Need for attention from peers or adults
Anger or stress
Depression, frustration or confusion (emotional states)
Power/control
Intimidation
Sensory under- or overstimulation
Request to obtain something (i.e., food, activity, object, comfort, routine, social interaction)
Expression of internal stimulation (i.e., sinus pain, skin irritation, hunger)
Obsessional thoughts
Fear of failure
Fear related to self-esteem (i.e., loss of face, loss of perceived position)
Fear of object, person, or event, or relief of fear
Need to protect an irrational thought

Student Perspective Analysis (SPA)

To the Interviewer:

Gather as much information as possible beforehand. Helpful information may include:

A. The student's daily schedule.
B. Teachers' names and the courses they teach.
C. Names and roles of other adults the student encounters.
D. Recent classroom assignments. It is often helpful to obtain samples of all types of assignments in all subject areas.

If you have no prior information, you may need to break up the interview into several different time periods and assess the whole day.

Discuss the reason for gathering information with the student. The following statement can be used to help the student understand the functional analysis, "The reason I'm asking these questions is so that we can learn about the things that are bothering you at school. Some of these things we may be able to fix. Other things we cannot change. Just because I'm listening to your answers does not mean that I can change all of these things. It is helpful for your teachers to know what is bothering you, because this information may help them understand you. When a person learns what is on someone's mind, it provides information about what someone is thinking. This can help individuals get along and respect each other, even if many things about the situation cannot be changed."

Please note that the form specifically suggests using the name of a school subject or the name of a teacher, rather than pronouns. Students with AS often find pronouns confusing; therefore, the questions will be clearer if you specifically use the teacher's name, rather than he/she or they.

SCHOOL

1. What is your first (next) class in school?
2. Who's your teacher?
3. Does <u>teacher's name</u> notice when you do a good job?
4. What does <u>teacher's name</u> do that tells you you've done a good job?
5. Do you think <u>teacher's name</u> likes you?
6. What does <u>teacher's name</u> do to show you he/she likes you?
7. Do you usually work alone or with others?
8. What kinds of things do you do alone?
9. What kinds of things do you do with others?
10. Which do you prefer?
11. Is the work difficult or easy?

Figure 3.2. *Student perspective analysis.*

12. What is the easy part of the schoolwork?
13. What part of schoolwork don't you like in <u>class or subject name</u>?
14. If you could change one thing about <u>class or subject name</u>, what would that be?
15. Name one easy thing in <u>subject name</u> class.
16. What is one thing you are good at in <u>subject name</u> class?
17. Do you have any problems with other students in <u>teacher's name</u> class?
18. Which students do you have problems with?
19. Tell me about the problem(s).
20. What would help the situation?
21. Do you always sit in the same seat?
22. Do you like where you are sitting? Why or why not?
23. How does <u>teacher's name</u> let you know what the homework is?
24. Does <u>teacher's name</u> make any changes that bother you?
25. Can you think of anything <u>teacher's name</u> does that bothers you? What?
26. Are there any things in the classroom that bother you a lot? (noises, smell, light, temperature, etc.)
27. Do you have enough time to do what <u>teacher's name</u> asks?
28. Do you have enough time to switch activities in <u>subject name</u> class?
29. Do you have enough time to get your work done?
30. Rank your classes (including bus, lunch) in order, with 1 being the best and __ being the worst. (Give the student a list of all classes and activities to include.)

RANK	CLASSES

31. Rank your teachers and other adults you see at school in order, with 1 being the best and __ being the worst. (Give the student a list of teachers and adults to include.)

Figure 3.2. *(continued)*

RANK	TEACHERS' NAMES

BUS

(NOTE: You may need to conduct two interviews – one for the morning bus ride and the other for the afternoon bus ride.)

32. Who is your bus driver?

33. Does <u>bus driver's name</u> like you? Dislike you?

34. What does the bus driver do that tells you he or she likes/doesn't like you?

35. Do you sit in the same seat every day?

36. Does anyone sit in the seat next to you? Who?

37. Are there students on your bus whom you like? Who?

38. Do you ever talk to them?

39. What do you talk about?

40. What do they talk about?

41. Are there students on the bus whom you do not like? Who?

42. Why don't you like them?

43. Do you like riding the bus? Why or why not? (If no, question further.)

LUNCH

44. What time do you eat lunch?

45. Do you always sit in the same seat?

46. Who do you like to sit with at lunch?

47. Is there anyone you do not like to sit with at lunch? Who? Why?

48. Do you have enough time to eat lunch?

49. Do you like lunchtime?

50. Does the noise or other parts of the cafeteria bother you?

51. If you could change one thing about lunchtime, what would it be?

Thanks to Dena Gitlitz for her invaluable assistance in the development of this interview form.

Figure 3.2. *(continued)*

Several functional assessment instruments are also available to help teachers and parents identify behavior triggers or functions. These include *Motivation Assessment Scale* (Durand & Crimmins, 1992); *Problem Behavior Questionnaire* (Lewis, Scott, & Sugai, 1994); and *Student-Assisted Functional-Assessment Interview Form* (Kern, Dunlap, Clarke, & Childs, 1994).

Develop and Implement a Behavioral Intervention Plan

Once functional assessment data have been collected, reviewed, and analyzed, the team must assimilate the information to gain a thorough understanding of the cause of behavior(s). This process is important because typically there is a pattern in the occurrence of the behavior. Once this pattern is identified, effective interventions can be designed and presented in a behavioral intervention plan. This plan includes a written description of specific interventions to be used with the student to promote behavioral, social, and academic success. In addition, the persons who will be responsible for implementing the plan must be listed. The behavioral intervention plan is mandated by the Individuals with Disabilities Education Act (IDEA, 1997) for students with problem behaviors.

Beyond solving an immediate situation, understanding a behavior and implementing a plan can also help teachers and parents be proactive. For example, in planning for the next school year, the intervention can be implemented as a part of the student's program prior to the behavior becoming an issue.

Collect Data and Follow up to Analyze the Effectiveness of the Plan

To ensure success, the effectiveness of the intervention outlined in the behavioral intervention plan must be monitored. To do so, a plan for data collection must first be established. Educators and parents should meet according to a predetermined schedule to compare the student's baseline data to intervention data and thereby determine the effectiveness of the intervention. If successful, the plan may need to be continued, possibly with modifications and adaptations. On the other hand, if the intervention is not as effective as hoped, it may be necessary to reexamine the behavior function and subsequently develop and implement a new behavioral intervention plan.

Summary

A thorough diagnostic assessment can help provide insight into the adolescent with AS. Curriculum-based, formal, and informal measures play a significant role in determining what the student knows and how she learns. If behavioral issues are a concern, functional assessment can yield important information about the individual's environments and demands. Sometimes it is difficult for others to understand why particular issues are problematic for individuals with AS. For this reason, it is important to understand the student's perspective as noted in this chapter. Careful observation of situations from the student's viewpoint provides invaluable assistance in structuring appropriate curricular and social experiences for adolescents with AS.

CHAPTER 4

Supports for Students with Asperger Syndrome in Middle and High School

Traditional middle and high school programs are problematic for many youths with AS.

As discussed in Chapter 1, compared to elementary schools, larger school size, departmentalized teaching, higher expectations, more rigorous grading policies, and increased homework demands add substantially to the challenges normally associated with puberty, which typically sets in around this time and can cause all kinds of havoc to an otherwise happy and well-adjusted adolescent due to hormonal changes.

Anybody who has lived or worked with a teenager knows that these can be tumultuous times for any student – in behavior and general mood. For students with AS the challenges are intensified by their typical impairments in social skills, communication, and behavior/emotional regulation. There is no such thing as "the" school program for students with AS. Because each youth is different, it follows that each program must be different.

Persons with AS can be successful in a variety of settings from full participation in general education classes without a paraprofessional, to full participation with a paraprofessional or resource room support coupled with general classroom attendance, to self-contained classroom placement. Parents and teachers have found that magnet schools, small private schools, or homeschooling provide the structure many youths with AS need. As we pointed out in Chapter 3, creating a program for a student with AS requires knowing her needs and creating a balance between her academic content needs, social needs, and stress/anxiety level.

Program needs change rapidly – perhaps even across semesters. When she started sixth grade, Julie participated in all general education classes with paraprofessional support. Academically, she could meet the requirements of the assigned schoolwork. However, she was distracted by noise and movement in the classroom and therefore required extra time to complete assignments. Julie also had difficulty being flexible. If she was expecting one assignment and another was given, she became anxious. Unplanned activity changes often resulted in withdrawal – she frequently reported being "paralyzed from doing anything" at these times. On occasion, her anxiety resulted in a meltdown.

To help Julie succeed and feel better about herself, a variety of strategies were put in place. But none was effective enough to make her days successful. Full inclusion with paraprofessional support was not working. Consequently, her school team (Julie's general and special education teachers; paraprofessional; support personnel, including a speech/language pathologist and psychologist; and administrators) and her parents developed a model that revolved around her resource room. Julie began her school day in the resource room and received the majority of her coursework there. She gradually began to attend general education classes, one at a time, as she felt comfortable. By the end of the school year, Julie was spending four hours in general education classes and three hours in the resource room. For Julie, this was a successful program.

We believe that no one model is best. Although it is currently popular to support the general education environment as the primary placement for students with disabilities, we do not. Instead, we support the model that works best for each student. In developing an individualized program, we see the following as goals for students with AS in middle and high school:

- to learn social skills and engage in social interactions
- to gain daily living skills
- to understand self, particularly as it relates to sensory and emotional needs
- to learn problem-solving skills
- to learn academic content

Depending on the youth, some of these skills may be the principal obligation of the school, while others would more naturally fall to the responsibility of parents. The school team, parents, and the student with AS should work together to make this determination.

What follows is a myriad supports that have been found useful for helping individuals with AS meet the challenges of middle and high school. Most likely, no one student will need all these accommodations and modifications in order to be successful. However, many teens with AS will require several selections from this menu.

In addition to being *individualized,* all the suggested modifications share two specific commonalities: *structure* and *predictability.* The structure provided by each support helps the student develop a routine or identify a specific place and time for an activity or assignment. With these modifications, the student always knows what he is expected to do, the order in which activities will occur, what comes next, and that teacher and parent expectations match his skill level. Predictability is also ensured. That is, if the modifications are clearly communicated, the adolescent will be able to determine by himself what he is to do.

Another component should be introduced into these commonalities: *flexibility.* Flexibility is not the opposite of structure or predictability, although intuitively it may seem so. We speak of *flexible structure* and *flexible predictability* to accommodate student needs. For example, the teacher has planned a lesson in science. Typically, the student knows what is expected and knows what to do. However, upon seeing the youth enter class one day, the teacher notices a high degree of anxiety in his face and overall appearance. As a result, she quickly decides to change the planned routine. The student who was otherwise going to participate in the group experiment, for example, may be given the option to (a) go to home base before beginning the experiment, (b) complete the experiment with only one other person, or (c) watch the experiment without actually participating. Such flexibility is needed because the student's needs have changed, if only momentarily. In this case, his need to de-stress overrules completing an activity in the planned manner. As this case illustrates, a successful program for an adolescent with AS is based on individualization, structure, predictability, and flexibility.

Within the real world of families and schools, the chronology of this and the next chapter in the book is reversed. That is, the supports detailed in this chapter are, of course, part of the overall transition planning, which is discussed in detail in Chapter 5. For the sake of continuity, however, we elected to present the supports first, followed by the "mechanics" of transition planning. Major topics to be discussed include academic modifications, modifications for unstructured and less structured times of the school day, environmental supports, and social supports. In addition, strategies that provide stabilization for students in crisis are presented.

Academic Modifications

Many students with AS need academic modifications that provide the predictability and structure that make learning less stressful. Several strategies used with students with mild-to-moderate disabilities (i.e., learning disabilities) prove helpful as academic supports. In addition, techniques highlighted in the literature on gifted students are appropriate for some students with AS. Specific modifications discussed here include: (a) priming, (b) classroom assignment modifications, (c) notetaking, (d) graphic organizers, (e) enrichment, and (f) homework.

Priming

Priming is an intervention that introduces information or activities prior to their use or occurrence (Wilde, Koegel, & Koegel, 1992). The purposes of priming are to (a) familiarize the youth with the material before its use; (b) introduce predictability into the information or activity, thereby reducing stress and anxiety; and (c) increase the student's success.

In priming, the actual materials that will be used in a lesson are shown to the student the day, the evening, or even the morning before the activity is to take place, and the student is reinforced for attending to the material. In some cases, priming occurs right before the activity, such as when a peer mentor overviews what will take place during the science experiment immediately prior to the beginning of science class. Priming can occur either in the classroom or at home. It can be done by a parent at home or by a paraprofessional, a resource teacher, or a trusted peer at school.

Wilde and colleagues (1992) recommend that the actual teaching materials such as a worksheet or textbook be used in priming. However, in some cases, we have been successful at priming using a list or a description of the activities to take place. For example, priming sessions with Heather consist of reviewing index cards that list what she will be doing the next day in each of her classes. Each index card lists the reading assignment, the number and type of questions she will have to answer followed by an example, the activity itself and how it will occur (in a small group of peers or individually) and finally her responsibilities for each class.

Priming is most effective when it is built into the student's routine. Yet, priming is not teaching, correcting or testing. To be effective, it should occur in an environment that is relaxing and given by a primer who is patient and encouraging. Finally, priming sessions should be short, providing a brief overview of the academic expectations in each class or activity.

Classroom Assignments

Student strengths and concerns dictate the content and format of assignments. Some students need additional time to complete tasks. For others, tasks may need to be shortened or the number of problems may have to be reduced. This can often be accomplished easily without drawing undue attention to the student. For example, when reducing the number of math problems assigned to the whole class, on the assignment sheet given to the student with AS, the teacher can simply circle the problems he must complete.

With the increased reading demands in middle and high school, it is important to evaluate the amount of reading the student with AS is assigned. For some subjects such as social studies and English, the reading load is extremely heavy. Students with AS, who sometimes read slowly and cannot discern relevant from irrelevant information, spend an inordinate amount of time concentrating on facts that will not be tested and are considered unimportant. Highlighted texts and study guides help these students maximize their reading time. Teachers should also consider identifying precisely which information the student is responsible for.

A model of what is expected on assignments or a specific list of criteria for grading assignments is also helpful. For example, if an essay on the Revolutionary War will be graded on neatness and spelling as well as content, this must be spelled out for the student. A model of an "A" paper and a "C" paper highlighting the differences between the two can also help the student be more successful.

Because handwriting is a challenge for many students with AS, the teacher should offer a variety of ways to demonstrate mastery. This includes verbal responses instead of written essays; using the computer instead of a pen or pencil; and completing a multiple-choice rather than a short-answer test. Student-developed projects may also allow demonstration of mastery. For example, a student can show content mastery by developing a timeline of events leading to the Civil War. Winebrenner (2001) has compiled an assortment of acceptable student projects that can be substituted for a traditional paper-pencil assignment (see Table 4.1).

Table 4.1
Acceptable Alternative Student Projects

---

1. Create a game for others to play to learn the information.
2. Create a radio or television broadcast or a video production.
3. Write a diary or journal of an important historical event or person; write a speech a person might have given at the time.
4. Write a song, rap, poem, advertisement, or jingle.
5. Create a travel brochure for another country or planet.
6. Write a script for a play or a mock trial.
7. Write a how-to manual for those who need instruction on how to do or use something.
8. Create a chart or poster to represent a synthesis of material.
9. Working with several other students, create a panel discussion about a topic of a certain historical time period or about how different historical figures might react to a problem of today.
10. Create an invention to fulfill a personal or social need.
11. Make a model; describe its parts and the functions of each.
12. Survey others; transfer your data to a chart or graph.

From *Teaching Gifted Kids in the Regular Classroom: Strategies and Techniques Every Teacher Can Use to Meet the Academic Needs of the Gifted and Talented* (p. 148), by Susan Winebrenner, 2001. Used with permission from Free Spirit Publishing Inc., Minneapolis, MN: 800/735-7323; www.freespirit.com.

Notetaking

Many students with AS have difficulty when required to take notes in class. Often motor problems preclude getting important content onto paper. In addition, some students have difficulty listening and writing at the same time. They can do both, but not together. Teachers can aid student learning by providing the following:

1. A teacher-developed complete outline that includes the main ideas and supporting details
2. A teacher-developed skeletal outline that includes the main ideas and provides spaces for the student to fill in supporting details as these are discussed in class
3. A peer-constructed outline developed by a fellow student using carbon paper or a photocopier
4. Outlining software that allows the computer-adept student to take notes on main ideas and details

Before any of these suggestions is implemented, teachers need to determine whether the student with AS knows how to identify main ideas and supporting details. Quite often these skills are not directly taught, but assumed to be in place when students reach middle school.

The first step in instruction is to teach the student to identify main ideas and details in familiar written material. It is recommended that written rather than oral material be used because it is static and allows for visual review. In addition, familiar materials allow the student to focus on learning how to outline rather than on understanding new content.

Once this step has been accomplished, students can begin the progression from using a teacher-developed complete outline to a skeletal outline. As mastery occurs, students gradually take more and more responsibility for outlining. The teacher facilitates this growing independence by teaching the student to recognize direct verbal cues such as *"The first main idea is ..."* or *"There are three details to remember. The first is ..."* When the student is proficient at this level, the teacher instructs on the use of indirect verbal cues (i.e., *"You need to remember ..." "The first battle of the Revolutionary War ..."*) (Kasselman & Myles, 1988; Myles & Simpson, 1998).

Some students may not be able to progress past the skeletal outline stage. In such cases, providing the materials needed, making outlining software available, or using peer-developed notes are viable ways of helping the student learn. In some classes, tape recording the lectures is beneficial.

Graphic Organizers

Graphic organizers are visual supports that organize content material in a way that makes it easier to understand. Used properly, they highlight important concepts and facts as well as display the relationship between them. That is, these strategies arrange key terms to show their relationship to each other, presenting abstract or implicit information in a concrete manner. Particularly useful with content area material such as social studies, literature, and science, graphic organizers can be used before, during or after reading a selection, either as an advance organizer or as a measure of concept attainment following reading.

Graphic organizers enhance the learning of students with AS because:

1. They are visual, and this modality is often a strength.
2. They are static; they remain consistent and constant.
3. They allow for processing time; the student can reflect on the material at his own pace.
4. They present abstract information in a concrete manner (Myles & Southwick, 1999).

Several types of graphic organizers exist. Bromley, Irwin-DeVitis, and Modio (1995) identified four basic types: (a) hierarchical, (b) conceptual, (c) sequential, and (d) cyclical. *Hierarchical organizers* highlight a main idea and subtopics in a linear fashion. *Conceptual graphic organizers* are often used to describe characters' actions and motivations. They begin with a concept, event or idea, with subtopics branching out from the central theme. Timelines are examples of *sequential organizers*. They can illustrate chronological order as well as cause and effect. Finally, *cyclical organizers*, as their name suggests, illustrate a series of events that have no beginning, middle or end. Scientific concepts, such as the water cycle and how the heart pumps blood through the body, are often visually represented in this manner. Figure 4.1 provides examples of graphic organizers that may be effective for children and youth with Asperger Syndrome.

Cyclical Graphic Organizer

Water collects in oceans,
lakes and rivers

The water travels
downhill
in rivers to reach
the ocean

Surface water in oceans,
lakes and rivers
is heated by the sun's
energy and evaporates,
becoming a gas known
as water vapor

Some of the precipitation is
absorbed by plants, some sinks
into the ground, while the rest
flows as runoff into rivers

Water vapor is carried
by the wind and
condenses when it
reaches cold air

This precipitation falls to
the earth in the form of
rain or snow

The condensed
vapor forms clouds

When clouds become
overloaded, they release
moisture as precipitation

Adapted from: Time-Life Books. (1997). *Time Life student library: Planet earth.*
Alexandria, VA: Author. *Developed by Cindy Van Horn.*

Figure 4.1. *Samples of graphic organizers.*

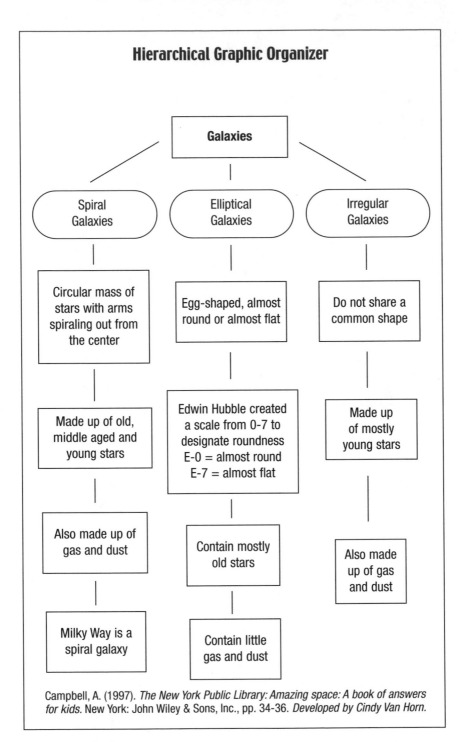

Figure 4.1. *(continued)*

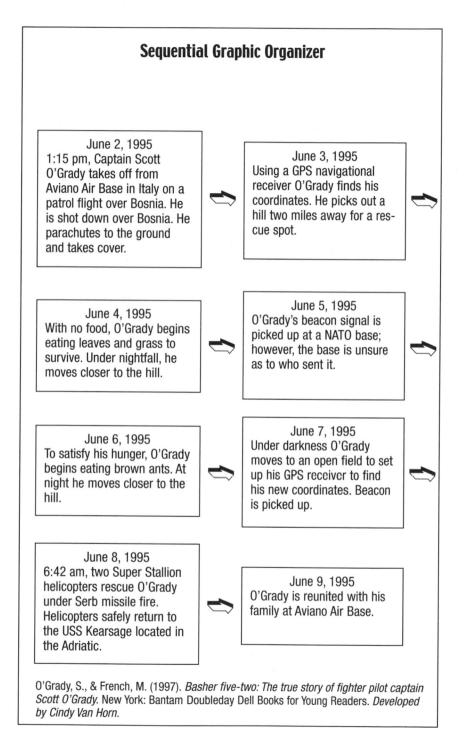

Sequential Graphic Organizer

> **June 2, 1995**
> 1:15 pm, Captain Scott O'Grady takes off from Aviano Air Base in Italy on a patrol flight over Bosnia. He is shot down over Bosnia. He parachutes to the ground and takes cover.

> **June 3, 1995**
> Using a GPS navigational receiver O'Grady finds his coordinates. He picks out a hill two miles away for a rescue spot.

> **June 4, 1995**
> With no food, O'Grady begins eating leaves and grass to survive. Under nightfall, he moves closer to the hill.

> **June 5, 1995**
> O'Grady's beacon signal is picked up at a NATO base; however, the base is unsure as to who sent it.

> **June 6, 1995**
> To satisfy his hunger, O'Grady begins eating brown ants. At night he moves closer to the hill.

> **June 7, 1995**
> Under darkness O'Grady moves to an open field to set up his GPS receiver to find his new coordinates. Beacon is picked up.

> **June 8, 1995**
> 6:42 am, two Super Stallion helicopters rescue O'Grady under Serb missile fire. Helicopters safely return to the USS Kearsage located in the Adriatic.

> **June 9, 1995**
> O'Grady is reunited with his family at Aviano Air Base.

O'Grady, S., & French, M. (1997). *Basher five-two: The true story of fighter pilot captain Scott O'Grady*. New York: Bantam Doubleday Dell Books for Young Readers. *Developed by Cindy Van Horn.*

Figure 4.1. *(continued)*

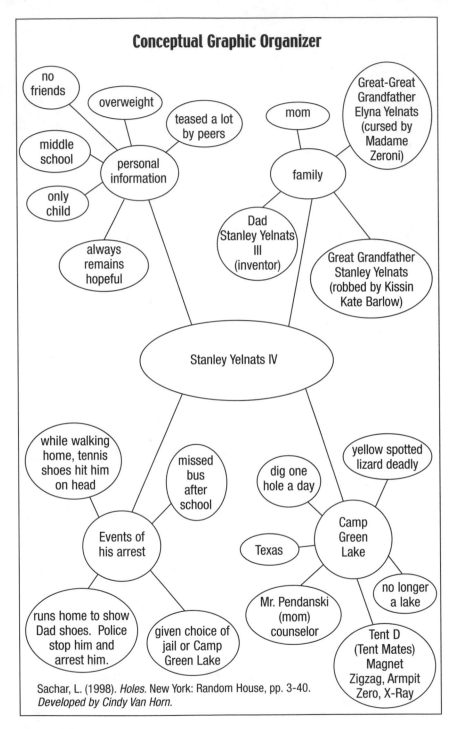

Figure 4.1. *(continued)*

Enrichment

Too often the talents of individuals with AS are ignored amidst a focus on areas of need. Research has shown that a greater percentage of students with AS have IQs in the superior or very superior range than found in the general population (Barnhill et al., 2000). How can we provide enrichment when the student has other skill areas that need to be addressed? Reis, Burns, and Renzulli (1992) suggest *compacting* to guide enrichment. Compacting means identifying student competencies and subsequently allocating time that would otherwise be devoted to those competencies to enriching activities.

Winebrenner (2001) used compacting with James, age 11, who was gifted in language arts, writing, grammar, and reading. She first pretested him on concepts that were to be taught in each area. As James demonstrated that he knew the concepts, he was assigned an alternate activity that he could engage in while other students were learning the previously mentioned tasks. The alternate activity was in the area of his interest – the human body. James' activity consisted of writing a book entitled "The Anatomy, Physiology, and Cetera of the Human Body" (Winebrenner, 2001, p. 42)!

Learning contracts can often be used effectively with or without compacting to individualize learning opportunities while maintaining control and accountability over content. As with compacting, students use the learning contract when the teacher is teaching content on which the student has pretested successfully. According to Winebrenner (2001), the learning contract specifies enrichment activities along with special instructions such as a timeline for completion and a list of materials needed in order to complete the activity, such as using the computer instead of paper and pencil. Alternative ways of demonstrating mastery may also be a part of the learning contract.

Finally, the contract also contains working conditions. Winebrenner suggests that the following be considered as working conditions, modified to fit specific student needs.

1. Stay on task at all times with the alternate activities you have chosen.
2. Don't talk to the teacher when the teacher is teaching.

Contract with Problem-Solving Focus

Student's Name: _____

___ Make tables or graphs	___ Work backwards
___ Make pictures	___ Act it out
___ Make diagrams	___ Use objects; use manipulatives
___ Find a pattern	___ Use logical reading
___ Estimate first, check later	___ Simplify the problem
___ Create an organized list	___ Write an equation

Extension Options

Create story problems for the class to do ___ ___ ___ ___ ___

Choose a method from the top of the contract; create 4-6 problems at different levels of difficulty ___ ___ ___ ___ ___

Study a math textbook from a higher grade level that is different from the adopted text; find and record problems that require specific problem-solving methods; name the methods ___ ___ ___ ___ ___

Select a problem that our school is experiencing; apply several of the methods listed above to solve it ___ ___ ___ ___ ___

Apply several of the methods to solve a personal problem. Help another student to understand a problem-solving method ___ ___ ___ ___ ___

Create an activity related to problem-solving ___ ___ ___ ___ ___

_____   _____
Teacher's signature   Student's signature

From *Teaching Gifted Kids in the Regular Classroom: Strategies and Techniques Every Teacher Can Use to Meet the Academic Needs of the Gifted and Talented* (p. 57), by Susan Winebrenner, 2001. Used with permission from Free Spirit Publishing Inc., Minneapolis, MN: 800/735-7323; www.freespirit.com.

Figure 4.2. *Learning contract for problem solving.*

3. When you need help and the teacher is busy, ask someone else who is also working on the alternate activities.
4. If no one else can help you, continue to try the activity yourself until the teacher is available or move on to another activity until the teacher is free.
5. Use "6-inch voices" when talking to each other about the alternate activities. These are voices that can be heard no more than 6 inches away.
6. Never brag about your opportunities to work on the alternate activities.
7. If you must go in and out of the room, do so soundlessly.
8. If you are going to work in another location, stay on task there, and follow the directions of the adult in charge.
9. Don't bother anyone else.
10. Don't call attention to yourself. (p. 51)

Working conditions as well as how to use the learning contract need to be taught to the student. A sample learning contract for problem solving appears in Figure 4.2.

Homework

Numerous challenges are inherent in assigning homework for students with AS. Attending a day of school is extremely stressful for these students. Therefore, stress level needs to be taken into account when deciding whether or not to assign homework to a given student. Often homework requirements are lessened or waived for students to allow them to focus on "de-stressing" and relaxing when they get home from school. Also, parents sometimes use after-school hours to provide practice in social skills learned at school and to follow up on individual student interests.

Even when it has been determined that assigning homework will have the intended benefits, educators and families often find it challenging to devise supports, adaptations, and systems for getting the information about homework assignments home. The most commonly reported homework problems include:

- The student did not write down the homework assignment.
- The student wrote down only part of the assignment.
- The student does not remember or know the details about the assignments that were given verbally in class.

- The materials necessary for completing the assignment did not come home with the youth.

There are a number of reasons why these types of problems occur. First, the visual-motor task of copying down information from the board or an overhead transparency may be difficult. As mentioned, handwriting is difficult for many students with AS. Further, teachers often give auditory details about an assignment at the same time students are to write down the assignment. But many students with AS cannot write and attend to other stimuli at the same time. Finally, the student may not think about the "global" requirements of the assignment, such as the materials needed, unless specifically taught to list the materials and place them on a to-do list of things to complete and materials to gather at a specific time at school, before leaving to go home.

For these reasons, it is necessary, in many instances, to implement numerous adaptations to ensure successful completion of homework. The school team and parents also need to identify key starting points for teaching the student with AS the skills needed to successfully complete homework. The Homework Checklist in Figure 4.3 helps ensure that homework gets home and is completed, and turned in.

Getting the homework assignment home is only one third of the challenge. The other two thirds consist of (a) getting the homework completed and (b) turning it in at school on time. At home, students need a designated place and time to complete homework. The place should be free from distractions but allow easy access so adults can monitor progress. Some parents report that their adolescents need time to relax immediately after school. If these students are given leisure time alone as soon as they get home, they can often complete homework successfully. Other parents report that their teenagers must complete homework as soon as they leave school. Otherwise, they say, their kids' momentum dies. Once this happens, both parties are frustrated – parents who want the homework done right away and teens who can't seem to get motivated to start the task.

As youths begin their homework, they or their parents often realize that they do not completely understand the assignment. A schoolwide homework hotline or peer network can help clarify ambiguities. One parent requested that her daughter's teachers

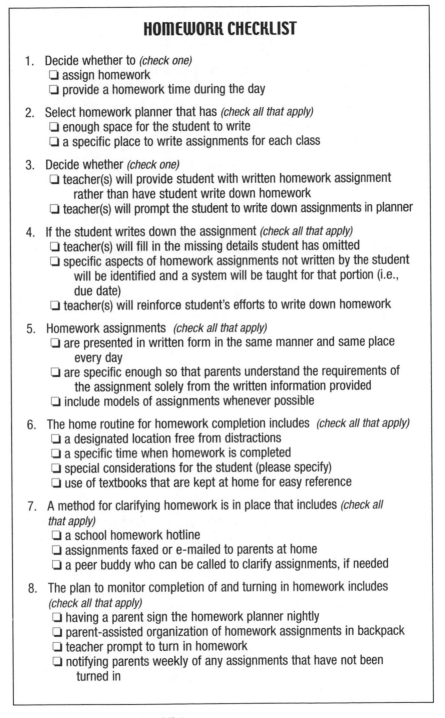

HOMEWORK CHECKLIST

1. Decide whether to *(check one)*
    - ❏ assign homework
    - ❏ provide a homework time during the day

2. Select homework planner that has *(check all that apply)*
    - ❏ enough space for the student to write
    - ❏ a specific place to write assignments for each class

3. Decide whether *(check one)*
    - ❏ teacher(s) will provide student with written homework assignment rather than have student write down homework
    - ❏ teacher(s) will prompt the student to write down assignments in planner

4. If the student writes down the assignment *(check all that apply)*
    - ❏ teacher(s) will fill in the missing details student has omitted
    - ❏ specific aspects of homework assignments not written by the student will be identified and a system will be taught for that portion (i.e., due date)
    - ❏ teacher(s) will reinforce student's efforts to write down homework

5. Homework assignments *(check all that apply)*
    - ❏ are presented in written form in the same manner and same place every day
    - ❏ are specific enough so that parents understand the requirements of the assignment solely from the written information provided
    - ❏ include models of assignments whenever possible

6. The home routine for homework completion includes *(check all that apply)*
    - ❏ a designated location free from distractions
    - ❏ a specific time when homework is completed
    - ❏ special considerations for the student (please specify)
    - ❏ use of textbooks that are kept at home for easy reference

7. A method for clarifying homework is in place that includes *(check all that apply)*
    - ❏ a school homework hotline
    - ❏ assignments faxed or e-mailed to parents at home
    - ❏ a peer buddy who can be called to clarify assignments, if needed

8. The plan to monitor completion of and turning in homework includes *(check all that apply)*
    - ❏ having a parent sign the homework planner nightly
    - ❏ parent-assisted organization of homework assignments in backpack
    - ❏ teacher prompt to turn in homework
    - ❏ notifying parents weekly of any assignments that have not been turned in

Figure 4.3. *Homework checklist.*

e-mail or fax assignments to her daily. That way, she could help her daughter meet homework requirements without any misunderstanding.

After the homework is finished, it must be organized for return to school, for example, by placing it immediately upon completion in the appropriate folder in the student's backpack. But there's yet another step. When the individual with AS arrives to class, having a routine for turning in homework on a visual support can serve as a reminder to the student. Also, a prompt from the teacher helps ensure that the homework is turned in and "the mission accomplished."

Modifications for Unstructured or Less Structured Times of the School Day

For many students with AS, the unstructured or less structured times of the day pose the greatest problems. Riding the bus, physical education, lunch, changing classes, changes in routine, and before-/after-school times are difficult because they pose complex social demands with minimal structure. In addition, these times are often accompanied by a marked increase in sensory stimuli such as noise, touch, and smell.

While problematic by themselves, all these factors increase the chance that the adolescent with AS will exhibit inappropriate behaviors and consequently be teased or bullied. The latter is of particular concern because individuals with AS are more likely to be teased, assaulted, or shunned than neurotypical children (Little, 2000). The suggestions in the following sections are designed to minimize students' chances of being victimized and to increase their ability to successfully manage less structured activities.

Transportation/Bus

For teens with AS, many aspects of getting to and from school by bus must be carefully considered to determine if adaptations or modifications are necessary to ensure an uneventful, safe ride for everyone. For example:

1. What is the noise level on the bus? On some buses the noise level

is high, causing sensory discomfort to the individual with AS.

2. What are the bus driver's rules and mannerisms? Often bus rules are part of the hidden curriculum (see Hidden Curriculum in this chapter). This may mean that the student with AS does not know how loudly she can talk and when talking is permitted.

3. Do bullies ride the bus? The bus ride may provide opportunities for teasing and ridicule that are often not noticed by the bus driver, whose primary focus is on driving safely.

Josiah rode the bus to and from school for the first two weeks of middle school. Each morning he would arrive at his home base and fall asleep. When his resource room teacher pointed this out to his mother, she decided that Josiah probably needed more sleep at night. But changing his bedtime did not impact Josiah's sleeping during home base. His teacher then suggested that rather than being tired, Josiah might be "shutting down" from stress and sensory overload. To check out this possibility, a paraprofessional, Mr. Chi, rode the bus two mornings and watched Josiah at the bus stop, on the bus, and starting his morning routine. Mr. Chi described the pushing and shoving among students that took place in getting on and off the bus, shouting that seemed to be a standard conversational protocol on the bus, slight teasing and physical jostling (Mr. Chi thought the students did this in fun, but was not sure whether Josiah understood the intent), and the bumpy ride on the bus. Mr. Chi confirmed that by the time Josiah got to school, he had endured about one hour of stress and clear sensory overload. No wonder, then, that he was shutting down when he finally arrived at a quiet, safe place. Josiah's early morning sleeping stopped suddenly when his dad started driving him to school.

Not all adolescents with AS have problems riding the bus. However, if the youth does ride the bus, decisions such as the following must be made by the school team and parents.

1. Is preferential seating needed (either near the bus driver or with a friend)?

2. Does the student know the bus driver's rules for conduct and talking?

3. Is the student aware of the consequences for breaking the bus driver's rules?

4. Does the student have the social skills necessary to talk effec-

tively with other kids while waiting for the bus and riding the bus?

5. Where does the student get assistance if he is being bullied or if he simply does not understand what he is supposed to do?

6. Does the bus driver know about Asperger Syndrome, in general, and the student's needs in particular?

7. Is an adult needed on the bus?

Physical Education

While most neurotypical teens enjoy physical education (PE) classes and sports programs as a diversion from sedentary academic classes, many youths with AS find this time of day stressful because of their poor motor skills and general difficulty with the concept of "team mentality" (Adreon & Stella, 2001). The structure in PE may also be confusing to the student with AS. Often the teaching staff operate under the assumption that all students know the rules for certain games, know where and how to line up, and understand how to win and lose graciously. They may also take for granted that everyone knows the language of PE.

Rita, a middle school student with AS, stood looking around as her PE teacher, in her no-nonsense voice, told everyone to line up for relay races. Misinterpreting Rita's disoriented behavior as non-compliance, the PE teacher ordered, "Rita, give me five." The PE teacher reported that she had to hide a smile and that the entire class laughed when Rita walked up to her to give her a "high five." Rita did not understand that she was supposed to do five pushups.

Based on an individual student's competencies, the school team should consider whether, and under what conditions, an adolescent should participate in PE. Some students with AS are successful in PE when the emphasis is on individual sports, such as cross-country running. In fact, one of the best "natural runners" in a local high school is a young man with AS. If the student does participate in PE, the teaching staff must ensure that she understands the structure, rules, and language of PE and that she is included in all activities. For example, the PE teacher may need to assign teams rather than allow for peer choices if it becomes apparent that the youth with AS is always selected last (Adreon & Stella, 2001).

Another aspect of PE – dressing out – can be problematic for teens with AS. Often the time allotted is not sufficient for these students to undress and dress. In addition, some students are extremely self-conscious about changing clothes in front of others. Finally, dressout time is a time when adolescents with AS are vulnerable to peer victimization because of awkward physical and/or social skills. Therefore, careful adult supervision during these times is warranted.

If the school team and parents decide that PE is not appropriate for a student, this time can be used for social skills instruction, home base, study hall, or enrichment activities in an academic subject in which the student excels. Some students remain active in PE by serving as score keepers, equipment managers, and so on.

Lunch

Like other unstructured or less structured times, lunch can be problematic for youths with AS. As in sports, social and sensory demands as well as time constraints can make this portion of the day challenging and stressful. In fact, many students with AS dread lunch, citing the smells and noise levels from the kitchen and the other students as bothersome. Trying to juggle eating and talking within a 20- to 30-minute period can also be difficult. Added to these issues is the stress of trying to use newly acquired social skills to interact with others (Adreon & Stella, 2001).

According to Odegaard and Heath (1992), the lunch period should be a comfortable time where students can eat, visit, and relax. If this is not the case, modifications may be needed. For example, if the student eats lunch in the designated lunchroom, she might need assigned seating with peer buddies near adult supervision and away from bothersome adolescents and extreme noise. Also, peers could assist the student in navigating the lunchroom, going through lunch lines, getting silverware, paying, and so forth. For some students with AS, lunch is a successful experience if they are allowed to leave the cafeteria as soon as they are finished eating. However, despite such modifications, some adolescents become stressed and overwhelmed at having to eat in the cafeteria. For them, an alternative location such as an empty classroom (preferably with peers) is a better option.

Changing Classes

Passing time between classes causes great apprehension for many students with AS, given the limited time they have to get to their lockers, open them, decide what materials they need, gather these materials, and then make their way to the next class on time. Often it is the idea that they have only a limited period in which to accomplish something that causes stress and frustration, rather than an actual lack of ability to complete the necessary tasks. Indeed, feeling rushed sometimes puts these students at a "standstill" (Adreon & Stella, 2001). The very nature of passing time between classes is at odds with what many of us know about AS – "Twice the time, half as much done" (Adreon & Gitlitz, personal communication, 2000). That is, adolescents with AS need more time than their neurotypical peers to accomplish tasks.

The school halls during passing time are chaotic. Often there does not seem to be enough room to accommodate everybody milling around. Students brush up against each other in their attempts to get where they are going, which can be misinterpreted as pushing and shoving and lead to frustration or even angry confrontation between students, especially given the sensory issues of many adolescents with AS.

> **... Passing time between classes causes great apprehension for many students with AS.**

A variety of modifications can make these transitions less frustrating. Early or late release from classes, preferably with a peer (for social reasons), allows the student with AS to move from class to class more successfully. The peers who accompany the student can help navigate the best route, open lockers, and organize materials. Some students may require a larger locker to compensate for poor organizational skills. Others may need another method than a combination lock to secure the locker because of fine-motor difficulties. Visual supports (see Environmental Supports in this chapter) also make passing time easier. In addition, a five-minute warning from the teacher that the class is coming to an end can make the transition more predictable.

Even with modifications, some adolescents cannot tolerate multiple class changes during the day. As mentioned, this is typically related to other issues than just the passing time itself. For example, students may have trouble adjusting to new rules, new routines, and new teacher expectations in each class. If the student is experiencing stress or frustration even with the supports suggested in this chapter, the school team and parents must consider whether the student's day needs to be structured in such a way that fewer passing times occur. For example, the student may have two science periods in the same classroom back to back or may attend a resource room for some periods during the day.

Changes in Routine

Even when care is taken to ensure that routines are in place and that students know and understand them, sometimes routines are disrupted. To accommodate schedule changes, parents and the team must determine whether and how to prepare the adolescent with AS for assemblies, fire drills, guest speakers, or seating changes. One routine disruption – the substitute teacher – merits special attention. If the student experiences problems when there is a substitute teacher, arrangements may be made for him to remain with a familiar teacher, spend the day in home base, or complete his work in the library or the computer lab.

Before and After School

The time the student spends in school prior to the start of classes and the period between the last bell and when the student leaves school in the afternoon must also be considered to determine if modifications are needed. At Wilson Middle School, students begin to arrive at 7:00 a.m., but they cannot get into the hallways until 7:40. During this interval, the students congregate in the lunchroom, where there appears to be little structure. Students can sit on the tables (!), on the benches, or stand around and talk to each other. They are permitted to play table-top games (checkers, chess, paper football) that can be finished in a relatively short time. No wonder there is a lot of movement, and lots of noise.

For students with AS who have difficulty with less structured times such as these, several options are available:

1. Students can be assigned to a different location (preferably with peers).
2. Students can have preferential seating with a selected group of peers near adult supervision in the lunchroom.
3. Students can be dropped off at school at 7:40 so they can proceed directly to their lockers. Or they can be dropped off at 7:30 with early passing time to their lockers.
4. Students may need assigned activities, regardless of where they spend the early morning time. In addition, a card of conversation starters might be helpful for promoting social exchange.

When the last bell of the day rings, a similar situation occurs. After gathering their materials, some students wait in the lunchroom or other designated area to be picked up by parents or the bus. Modifications that make the early morning successful most likely will need to be repeated during the after-school time.

Environmental Supports

To enhance success in school for students with AS, the environment must be modified or enhanced to meet each individual's special needs. At the middle school and high school level, the goal is first to teach the student to recognize her need for environmental supports. Then the student must learn to request supports or implement acquired strategies. Environmental supports effective for adolescents with AS include (a) preferential seating, (b) organizational strategies, (c) home base, (d) safe person, (e) visual supports, and (f) the Travel Card.

Preferential Seating

Care should be taken when assigning desks to students with AS. Make sure the student's desk is placed so that the teacher can easily monitor the student's attention to task without calling undue notice to this precautionary measure. Also, do not place the youth near high-traffic areas (near the waste basket or pencil sharpener) or near windows, which provide opportunities for distraction. Sona Chadwick (personal communication, 2000) recommends placing carefully selected nondisabled peers at least two deep in all directions from the student with AS. These students can cue the youth with AS to attend or to turn to the right page in the book or assignment.

Organizational Strategies

Lack of organizational strategies often prevents students with AS from demonstrating their full competence. For example, it is not uncommon to hear about adolescents with AS who have completed an assignment but weren't able to find it to turn it in on time. In addition to being able to locate assignments to be turned in, organization entails knowing which papers to keep and which ones to throw away. Organization also includes being able to open the locker and know where to find the notebook needed for biology, for example. In addition, adolescents need to be able to organize their backpacks; books, notebooks and folders; pens, pencils and other school supplies; ongoing projects; money for lunch; gym clothes; and so on.

Learning to develop timelines is an important organizational strategy for youths with AS. Timelines break assignments and other tasks into their component parts and set deadlines for their completion. Because individuals with AS often have difficulty with the concept of time, many think they can both read a novel and write a 10-page paper the night before it is due. Others cannot get started when they are given a complex task because they are unable to break it down into smaller pieces without assistance. The result is worry and frustration because the student did not have a strategy to begin and/or complete the task. Table 4.2 outlines some organizational supports for middle and high school students.

Home Base

A home base is a place in the school where the student can go to (a) plan or review the day's events, (b) escape the stress of the classroom, (c) prevent a meltdown, or (d) regain control if a tantrum, rage, or meltdown has occurred. The location is not important – the counselor's office, speech/language pathologist's room, or resource room can all serve as a home base (Myles & Simpson, 1998; Myles & Southwick, 1999). One student we know has his home base in

Table 4.2
Organizational Supports

School Supplies
1. Consider color-coded folders. A colored dot can be placed on the spine of textbooks that match the corresponding folder.
2. Consider a trapper keeper that contains all folders.
3. Have a section in the folder for papers going home and papers that need to return to school.
4. Keep pens and pencils in each folder.
5. If block scheduling is used, prepare a different set of organizational tools for each block. For example, on A day have an A backpack and an A day planner. On B day have a B backpack and a B planner.
6. Have a system in place to identify papers that can be discarded and/or taken home. Take these papers home daily.

Backpack
1. Use a multicompartment backpack. Have a separate section for school supplies, lunch money, folders, etc.
2. In addition to having pens and pencils with each folder, carry extras in the backpack.
3. Clean out backpack each evening.
4. Reload and organize backpack as soon as homework is completed.
5. Designate a place at home for storing the backpack.

Locker
1. Consider a backpack on wheels and eliminate the use of the locker.
2. Place materials in the locker in the order in which they will be needed. If the student takes books for two classes at once, encourage her to place them together in the locker. Consider placing a large rubber-band around the two books. (Note: Carry extra rubber-bands in the backpack.)

To-Do List and Timeline
1. Use a to-do list. Instructions include (a) crossing off completed items, (b) transferring items not yet completed to the next page, and (c) making a list of reminders (i.e., what special materials to bring to class; what books are needed from the library). The to-do list can be organized by subject.
2. For long-term projects, the to-do list can be a combination task analysis and timeline. Teach the student that each task in the project is written down along with its due date. As each step is completed, the student crosses it off.

From *Organizational supports* by D. Adreon, 2000. *Florida Asperger Syndrome Times.* Miami: University of Miami Center for Autism and Related Disabilities. *Special thanks to Cindy Griego for her suggestions.*

the custodian's office because of the rapport between the two. But regardless of its location, it is essential that the home base is viewed as a positive environment. Home base is not timeout! Also, it is not an escape from classroom tasks. The student takes her class work with her to home base.

Some students need home base to be scheduled as a regular part of their day. A home base at the beginning of the day can serve to preview the day's schedule, introduce and get familiar with changes in the typical routine, ensure that the student's materials are organized, or prime for specific subjects.

Home base can also be scheduled after particularly stressful activities or classes. Lunchtime is often difficult for Marco. The lunchroom is noisy and appears chaotic. Marco must be diligent to finish his lunch on time. He wants to talk with other kids during lunch, but most often his attempts to converse with the other students are unsuccessful. For all these reasons, Marco typically leaves lunch feeling mildly upset. To help him get ready for the rest of the day, he goes to home base before his social studies class. The resource room teacher in his home base helps him get organized for social studies and discusses with him some of the problems that may have occurred during lunch. Marco arrives in social studies about 10 minutes late each day. This means that he misses the opening activity, copying notes from the chalkboard, but knowing about his home base arrangement his social studies teacher has a copy of the notes waiting on his desk.

For students who do not like to arrive at class late or to leave class early because of a home base, an alternative approach is possible. One successful alternative involves having a peer accompany the youth with AS to or from home base. When using this option, always strive to select peers who (a) like the student with AS, (b) are a potentially good "friendship" match, and/or (c) hold a high status among others. Neurotypical kids, when offered to accompany a student with AS, usually jump at the opportunity. After all, who doesn't want to miss a bit of class? As a side benefit, the youth with AS and the neurotypical peer have opportunities to talk with each other on the way to and/or from home base. These social interactions are typically somewhat successful for the youth with AS because they are brief and both parties are attempting to listen and talk to each other.

Safe Person

A "safe person" is an adult in whom the youth with AS is comfortable confiding and being around. It is ideal if the safe person is the one who supervises home base. The role of the safe person can be multifaceted. In addition to helping complete home base activities, the safe person can (a) teach social skills, (b) interpret social situations, (c) listen and empathize, or (d) help the youth achieve emotional "readiness" for upcoming classes or activities.

This may include (a) providing sensory activities for the student (under the direction of an occupational therapist) (see *Asperger Syndrome and Sensory Issues: Practical Solutions for Making Sense of the World* by Myles et al., 2000, or *Tool Chest for Teachers, Parents, and Students* by Henry Occupational Therapy Services, 1998) or (b) helping the student adjust her "alertness" level using a curriculum such as the *How Does Your Engine Run* program (Williams & Shellenberger, 1996).

The specific role of the safe person depends on the needs of the student, the amount of time allotted for home base, and the qualifications of the adult. For example, if the student has developed a good rapport with the head custodian and wants to talk over social issues with him, the custodian would not be in charge of providing social skills or sensory activities. But with time and training, the custodian could help the youth with AS interpret social situations (see Social Skills Interpretation in this chapter). On the other hand, if the resource room teacher serves as the safe person, he or she can provide a full complement of social and sensory instruction.

Visual Supports

Visual supports help individuals with AS focus on the task at hand by clarifying, reminding, and directing. A variety of visual supports can be used to make life easier for the student with AS at the middle and high school level. Most adolescents do not want to appear different from their peers. Therefore, care should be taken when designing visual supports to ensure that (a) they are created in a such a way that everyone in the class uses them or (b) they are not obvious to any other students than the one for whom they are intended. When teachers begin to use visual supports such as those

Table 4.3
Visual Supports for Middle and High School Students with AS

Type of Support	Purpose	Location	Brief Description
Map of school outlining classes	-To assist the student in navigating school halls	-Taped or velcroed™ inside locker -Velcroed™ inside back cover of textbook or folder/notebook	To help orient and structure the student. This map shows the student where her classes are, the order in which they take place and times to visit her locker.
List of classes, room numbers, books and other supplies needed	-To aid the student in getting to class with needed materials	-Taped or velcroed™ inside locker -Velcroed™ inside back cover of textbook or folder/notebook	This list works well with students who have difficulty with maps. It lists the class, room number, supplies needed and when to go to the class.
List of teacher expectations and routines for each class	-To help the student understand the environment	-Velcroed™ inside front cover of text-book or folder/note-book -Placed on a key ring that is kept in pocket or on backpack	To reduce anxiety associated with routines and lack thereof, this visual support details the routine to be followed in the classroom (such as what the student is to do upon entering class and when and where to turn in homework), and outlines particular charac-teristics that can help the student get along in class (such as Mrs. Johnson does not permit talking with neighbors and likes two feet on the floor at all times; Mr. Thomas allows students to bring a bottle of water to class).

Table 4.3 *(continued)*
Visual Supports for Middle and High School Students with AS

Type of Support	Purpose	Location	Brief Description
Schedule of activities within the class	-To prepare the student for upcoming activities as well as assist in transition between activities	-Listed on the chalkboard or whiteboard	This list simply details what activities will occur during a given class. As each activity is completed, it can be erased, crossed out, or checked off. **Mr. Martin's 3rd Hour Spanish Class Activity Guideline Mon., March 5, 2001** ☐ Turn in homework assignment. Put it in the blue basket. ☐ Whole class lesson on Section 1, Chapter 4. ☐ Write homework assignment in your folder.
Outlines and notes from lectures	-To facilitate the student's understanding of content material	- Prepared by teacher in advance and placed on student's desk - Notes taken by peer during class using carbon paper or photocopied and handed out at the end of class -Tape recording of lecture with tape recorder placed near teacher and tape discreetly provided to the student at the end of class	Many students with AS have fine-motor difficulties that make it difficult for them to take notes. Others cannot take notes and listen at the same time. These supports alleviate these challenges and allow the student to focus on understanding the content.

Table 4.3 *(continued)*

Visual Supports for Middle and High School Students with AS

Type of Support	Purpose	Location	Brief Description
Sample models of assignments	-To help the student understand exactly what is required	-Prepared in advance by the teacher and given to the student discreetly. This can be an actual copy of an assignment that received an "A" grade	A model of assignments helps students be visually aware of format requirements. They can then concentrate on content.
List of test reminders	-To ensure that the student knows when a test occurs and what material will be covered	-Prepared in advance by the teacher and given to the student to allow sufficient time to study -Final reminder given the day before the test. Often presented on a colorful piece of paper and placed in the student's folder -A schoolwide homework hotline is helpful. If this is not available, a peer can serve as the homework hotline	A study guide that lists content and text-book pages covered in the test is helpful. It should include a timeline for studying and outlining content to be studied each night and the approximate time required to do so. The teacher assumes responsibility for developing it initially, but then works with the student to complete the task independently.

English Test
Thursday, April 26, 2001

- Monday, April 23, read Chapter 4, pages 75-93, in text (30 min.).
- Tuesday, April 24, outline the main ideas of the chapter – the theme (10 min.).
- Tuesday, April 24, list the main characters and their importance to the story (15 min.).

Table 4.3 *(continued)*

Visual Supports for Middle and High School Students with AS

Type of Support	Purpose	Location	Brief Description
List of schedule changes	- To ensure that the student is prepared for change	-Written on the chalkboard or whiteboard -Prepared in advance by the teacher (at least one day prior to activity) and given to the student to place in notebook. If the activity is one that the student is not familiar with, it should also include his behavioral responsibilities	This prompt helps students prepare for a change in routine. Including the student's responsibilities helps her complete the activity with minimal stress/anxiety.
List of homework assignments	-To assist the student in understanding requirements enough so that he can complete homework independently	-Prepared in advance and given to the student discreetly. This homework support should include all relevant information such as due date, items to complete, and format	Students with AS need written details of homework. Teachers often write on the board or overhead the basic elements of homework and supplement them verbally as students write down the assignment. This is not sufficient for students with AS.

Mr. Martin's 3rd Hour Spanish Class complete list and details of homework

Assignment Date: _____
Due Date: _____
The Assignment: _____

Page Number(s): _____

Table 4.3 *(continued)*
Visual Supports for Middle and High School Students with AS

Type of Support	Purpose	Location	Brief Description
Cue to use home base	- To prompt the student to leave class to lower her stress/anxiety level	- A small card, approximately the size of a business card, is carried by the teacher who discreetly places it on the student's desk when home base is needed	Students with AS often do not recognize that they are entering the cycle for a tantrum, rage, or meltdown. When the teacher recognizes the behaviors associated with the start of the cycle, she can use this card to prompt the student to leave the room. **Take A Break**

Sample visual supports developed by Rochelle Matthews.

outlined in Table 4.3, they often find that all students benefit. However, while they may benefit all students, visual supports are essential for students with AS.

Travel Card[3]

The Travel Card, first discussed by Jones and Jones (1995), is designed to (a) increase productive behavior in adolescents with AS across their many environments, (b) facilitate collaboration between teachers, (c) increase awareness among teachers of the goals the student is working on, and (d) improve home-school communication. Briefly, across the top the Travel Card lists four to five target behaviors the student is working on with a listing of the classes she attends along the left-hand side. At the end of each period, the teacher indicates whether the student performed the desired behaviors by marking a + (yes), 0 (no), or NA (not applicable) on the card.

At the end of the day, the positive notations are tallied and graphed. Points are accumulated toward a menu of reinforcers that have been jointly negotiated by the student and the adult responsible for the Travel Card. Initially, it is recommended that Travel Cards be used four days a week, with the fifth day used for reinforcement. The student may elect to receive a reinforcer right away or opt to place the points into a Travel Account that can be redeemed at a later time. Figure 4.4 shows a sample Travel Card for Rocky, a sixth-grade student with AS.

Target behaviors are selected for the student from several sources: (a) problem areas identified by general education teachers and parents, (b) objectives from the student's IEP, or (e) student self-evaluation.

An adult, typically a special educator or the student's case manager, assumes responsibility for developing and monitoring the Travel Card. After the target behaviors have been identified, the educator teaches a series of lessons on those behaviors. When the student demonstrates that she can perform a behavior in at least one setting, the behavior becomes a part of the Travel Card. Behaviors

---

[3] Contributed by Laura B. Carpenter, Auburn University, Montgomery.

Travel Card
Rocky

Date _____

Key   +=Yes   0=No   NA=Not Applicable

	Did student follow class rules?	Did student participate in class?	Did student complete assignments?	Did student turn in homework?	Teacher's initials
Reading					
Science					
Social Studies					
Study Skills					
English					
Spanish					
Bonus Points	Went to nurse after getting off bus?			Has assignment book?	

Total	+	0

Teacher Comments/Suggestions/Announcements:

Figure 4.4. *Travel card for Rocky.*

that are emerging or are demonstrated by a prompt are listed as bonus points. In this way, the student is motivated to practice a skill without being punished because it is still emerging. The special educator is also responsible for (a) collecting the Travel Card at the end of the day, (b) providing a new card each morning, (c) monitoring student behavior, and (d) communicating with teachers and parents on the effectiveness of the Travel Card. Table 4.4 lists the special educator's responsibilities for the Travel Card.

The student with AS also has Travel Card responsibilities. Because self-regulation of behavior is one of the prime objectives of the Travel Card, the student responsibilities emphasize this attribute. The ultimate goal is to have the student (a) carry the Travel Card to each class, (b) prompt each teacher to complete the card, (c) return the card to the special educator, (d) tally and graph points, and (e) select reinforcers (see Table 4.4). For most students with AS, this is a gradual process. It is recommended that Travel Card independence be initiated systematically, depending on student needs and functioning level.

Several options exist for introducing the Travel Card system. Initially, general education teachers may have to maintain the card, prompt the student to engage in the target behaviors, and ensure that the card is returned daily to the special educator. The Travel Card may be introduced in one setting, with other settings added as the student is successful.

The general educator's participation in the Travel Card program is also essential. Through the use of the Travel Card, the general educator can help the student generalize behaviors taught by a special educator or case manager. In addition, because the general educator is aware of the behaviors the student is working on, he or she can provide reinforcement when those behaviors occur (see Table 4.4 for the general educator's responsibilities).

As shown in Table 4.4, parents play another important role in the Travel Card program. They assist in identifying target behaviors; encourage the use of the behavior at home (when appropriate); reinforce behaviors exhibited in school; and communicate with school staff about how the adolescent reacts to the intervention.

Table 4.4
Travel Card Responsibilities

Special Educator

1. Identifies target behaviors with school team and parents.
2. Conducts an orientation on the Travel Card with school staff and parents.
3. Teaches target behaviors to the student.
4. Assesses student to determine if he can perform the behavior with teacher prompts. The student should know how to perform the target behavior in at least one setting with a prompt before being expected to perform it across multiple settings.
5. Teaches a series of short lessons to the student on the Travel Card system. This includes the penalty for falsifying teacher information (student loses all accumulated travel points).
6. Identifies reinforcers with student. The menu should consist of a variety of reinforcers that can be earned over a short time as well as some that are earned over an extended period.
7. Disseminates new Travel Cards at the beginning of each day.
8. Collects the Travel Card at the end of each day. Must make every effort to respond as soon as possible to any notes, concerns, or problems indicated on the Travel Card.
9. Continues to monitor and assess the student across multiple settings. Communicates student progress to other teachers and parents.
10. Makes changes in Travel Card as indicated by feedback from general educators, parents, and student.

Student

1. Demonstrates the targeted skills following instruction.
2. Demonstrates understanding and skills needed to carry the Travel Card.
3. Selects a menu of reinforcers with special educator.
4. Carries the Travel Card for the duration of the school day.
5. Asks the teacher at the end of each class to record a symbol on the Travel Card.
6. Leaves the Travel Card with the last teacher of the day. (The special educator collects the Travel Card from this person.)
7. Tallies and graphs Travel Card points.
8. Selects, on the fifth day, the Travel Card that is to be included in the student's portfolio or home communication.
9. Selects reinforcers based on number of Travel Card points earned or saves points in a Travel Account.

Table 4.4 *(continued)*
Travel Card Responsibilities

General Educator
1. Assists in identifying target behaviors for the Travel Card.
2. Attends an orientation on use of the Travel Card.
3. Shares progress and concerns related to existing target behaviors.
4. Prompts the student to perform target behaviors (early on) and provides written and verbal constructive feedback for each target behavior at the end of the teaching period.

Parent
1. Works with the school team to identify target behaviors.
2. Attends an orientation on the Travel Card. Orientation can occur during a parent conference, a parent organization meeting, or through written communication. An orientation that is offered both verbally and in writing is recommended.
3. Reinforces the youth for progress toward Travel Card behaviors.

Social Supports

The social challenges seen in most adolescents with AS make social supports absolutely essential to school success. It is important from the start to spell out for the student the social skills that will make life easier. Although some argue the value of instruction in this area because of the complexity of social skills, it is necessary to provide supports to students with AS so they do not make the same social errors repeatedly, are not ostracized socially, and maintain good self-esteem.

Particularly in school settings, certain social supports appear essential, including (a) understanding unwritten social rules, (b) making friends and meeting supportive peers, (c) having a base of skills to support social interaction, (d) having someone who can explain or interpret social situations that the student with AS did not understand or that did not occur as planned, and (e) understanding how sensory needs can impact interactions. These areas are discussed in the remainder of this chapter under the headings of (a) Hidden Curriculum, (b) Circle of Friends, (c) Social Skills Instruction, (d) Social Skills Interpretation, and (e) Sensory Issues.

As is the case with many of the other strategies and adaptations/modifications addressed in this book, in most cases, social supports have been implemented for the student with AS in the earlier grades. Nevertheless, this remains an important area in middle and high school, particularly during the transitioning process. Friends from grade school may not follow the student with AS to the same middle- or secondary-level school, making it necessary to make new friends. Also, generalization is often a problem for students with AS. Hence the need for constant mentoring and intercession as social situations demand.

Hidden Curriculum

The hidden curriculum is the set of rules that everyone in the school knows, but that no one has been directly taught (Bieber, 1994). The hidden curriculum includes such subtle elements as how to dress, how to act, what to do, what not to do and when, who to talk to, who to ignore, and so on. The hidden curriculum also includes knowing (a) teacher expectations, (b) teacher-pleasing behaviors, (c) students who potentially make good friends, (d) individuals who are likely to get you in trouble, (e) behaviors that attract positive attention from teachers and peers, and (f) behaviors that are considered negative or inappropriate by teachers and peers (Myles & Simpson, 1998, 2001).

It is imperative that the teen with AS understand her teachers' personalities and expectations. At that age, almost all youths have figured out their teachers by the end of the first week at school. For example, they know which teachers they can joke with, which teachers will not tolerate certain comments, which teacher allows late assignments, and which teacher does not grade quizzes closely. Simply by being in class and observing human nature, most youths understand what makes their teachers "tick."

However, this valuable survival information is usually not available to individuals with AS. We consider it absolutely necessary that students with AS acquire this information, and the only way they will learn it is through direct instruction. Someone, usually the safe person, must instruct the student on individual teachers' behaviors and expectations. Specifically, students need to know:
- How to tell when the teacher "means business"

- How to tell when the teacher is happy with the student's performance
- What the teacher does to communicate that he is angry
- Which teachers they can joke with and under what circumstances
- What tasks are most important to the teacher (such as tests vs. assignments)
- What upsets the teacher and/or what the teacher's "pet peaves" are
- What the rules are for talking in class
- How to ask questions during a lecture or lesson
- Who to see if they have a problem
- How to request help in each class
- When and how to turn in homework and class assignments
- How flexible the teacher is regarding late assignments
- Does the teacher allow students to negotiate due dates, how assignment is to be completed, where assignment can be completed, etc.
- Where to sit in class so there is easy access to the teacher
- What to do in individual classes if they do not have the right supplies or left their homework in the locker
- What to be doing in each class when the bell rings
- What the penalty is for turning in assignments late, being tardy, or missing supplies

Knowing the hidden curriculum is essential for youths with AS, as it can keep them out of trouble and help them make friends (Myles & Simpson, 1998, 2001). Every neighborhood, school, and community has a hidden curriculum, and it is a lack of awareness of these unspoken rules that often gets youths with AS in trouble (Myles & Simpson, 2001).

The youth with AS needs instruction in the hidden curriculum to ensure both social and academic success. Without formal hidden curriculum instruction, some have developed their own rules. Among the most noted published hidden curriculum items are those developed by Temple Grandin, a person with AS. Dr. Grandin's hidden curriculum includes identifying what she calls (a) really bad things, (b) courtesy rules, (c) illegal but not bad things, and (d) sins of the system. For example, she classifies slight speeding as illegal, but not bad. However, in order to be safe and not receive a speeding ticket, "slight speeding" has to be carefully defined (Grandin, 1999).

Kaitlin, in middle school, was very interested in word games and puns. One day in gym, as they were dressing out, a couple of students told Kaitlin that they had had been watching the planets and had just seen Uranus. They laughed and said, "Your anus. Get it!" Kaitlin thought it was a great joke and laughed too. But she did not receive the same response when she told the joke later during a science lecture on the planets. Kaitlin did not know the hidden curriculum item – "Do not tell jokes about body parts in class or to your teacher" – and subsequently got in trouble with her science teacher and was laughed at by fellow students. Hidden curriculum items that merit consideration appear in Table 4.5.

Circle of Friends

Some teens with AS are fortunate enough to belong to a small group of friends who look after each other. Developing a group of friends often makes the difference between success and failure for youths with AS.

Justin, a teen with AS, and his next-door neighbor, Tom, have been friends since third grade. Tom is popular with kids his own age and exhibits many teacher-pleasing behaviors. He is viewed as a good friend and a good student. Tom and Justin share many interests, including the Civil War, and have spent many hours together building a replica of battle sites in Justin's basement. For Tom, the Civil War is interesting; for Justin it is almost obsessive. Before knowing anything about AS, Tom liked Justin and saw him as a bright and funny friend. Although he noticed that Justin had problems getting along with other kids, Tom didn't have a problem with Justin. No one talked about Justin's AS until the sixth grade when he started having problems in his general education classes. Tom watched Justin's difficulty following teacher directions, getting to class on time, bringing the right supplies for each class, and knowing how to get along with other kids. When Tom talked to his mom about Justin's problems, she suggested that they both speak with Justin and his parents. Justin's parents were surprised at Tom's insights and explained their son's AS. With the support of both sets

---

Table 4.5
Sample Hidden Curriculum Items

BATHROOM

1. Don't write on the bathroom walls, especially when there is an adult in the bathroom.
2. For boys, don't talk to others in a restroom while you are urinating.
3. For girls, know which toilets you can sit on and which ones you should squat over.

SCHOOL

1. Don't bring tuna fish to school in your lunch – it smells and kids won't want to sit by you.
2. When walking up/down staircases, stay on the right so you are not walking against the traffic.
3. Don't look over someone's shoulder when he/she is checking e-mail.
4. Know which kids not to pick on or tease.
5. When you are taking a shower in gym class, do not sustain eye contact for very long or watch others take their showers.
6. Do not to pass gas, pick your nose, or scratch an itch of a private body part in any class.
7. Talk to teachers using a pleasant tone of voice because then they will respond to you in a more positive manner. They also like it if you smile every once in a while.
8. Rules change from teacher to teacher and it does not do any good to focus on the fact that it may not be fair.
9. When a teacher tells a student to stop talking, it is not a good idea to start talking to your neighbor since the teacher has already expressed disapproval of that action.
10. If you do something funny, it is usually only funny once. If you do it repeatedly, it makes you look silly and goofy and people might make fun of you.

RULES TO LIVE BY

Do not ...

1. ... interrupt others (especially teachers) when they are talking.
2. ... laugh when someone is crying.
3. ... talk loudly in a movie theater.
4. ... cut in line when buying tickets for an event.
5. ... grab somebody when you want him to dance with you.
6. ... laugh when someone is angry.
7. ... tell someone she is ugly.
8. ... literally jump in a lake when someone tells you to do so.
9. ... exclusively talk about your personal interests. Talk about something the other person is interested in too.

Table 4.5 (continued)
Sample Hidden Curriculum Items

---

10. ... try to sit in a chair that someone else is occupying – even if it is "your" chair.
11. ... argue or debate with a policeman – even if you are right.
12. ... touch a person's hair even if you think it is pretty.
13. ... correct someone's grammar when he is angry.
14. ... break laws – no matter your reason.
15. ... ask to be invited to someone's party.
16. ... tell someone that her house is much dirtier than it should be.
17. ... tell a person with a new puppy that the breed he bought has a terribly aggressive disposition.
18. ... tell a boy or girl that you like and are trying to get to know that he/she has bad breath.
19. ... do what actors do on television. Television shows are not the same as real life.

---

of parents, Tom and Justin agreed to a plan that Tom would kind of "look out" for Justin in the classes they had together. Justin could ask Tom questions and Tom would bring up any problems he saw. Both parents agreed that it was not Tom's job to make sure that Justin's day was successful. Tom's job was to be a student and a friend.

It is important to make sure that individuals with AS develop a social network as this does not come naturally to them. If the Circle of Friends concept is used, it is recommended that more than one teen be involved. Individuals who make up the Circle of Friends should be (a) high-status peers, (b) generally compliant with school rules, (c) socially astute, and (d) genuinely interested in (and, hopefully, like) the student with AS. Individuals who enjoy the way persons with AS look at life are excellent candidates for a Circle of Friends. Moreover, those who participate in the circle must value the person with AS, not merely placate and direct her (Myles & Simpson, 1998). It is sometimes easier to recruit young girls than boys to be in a Circle of Friends as they tend to be more nurturing and sensitive to the needs of others at this age. However, if high-status girls, such as cheerleaders, drill team members, or athletes, participate in a Circle of Friends, neurotypical boys will generally follow.

It is important to provide AS awareness training to ensure success in a Circle of Friends. While it is not important that the term "AS" be used, it is essential that the "friends" understand the individual with AS and how they can best become friends. Parents of the youth with AS should be involved in developing a Circle of Friends and any awareness training. Some parents include the teenager with AS in the awareness training. Others have made the opposite decision, asking the peer group not to say that they are a Circle of Friends. Some parents have even paid students to participate in Circle of Friends activities after school. However, it is preferable to facilitate relationships that have a chance to develop into true friendships.

Establishing a Lunch Bunch is one way of using a Circle of Friends. Lily, a middle school student with AS, participates in a Lunch Bunch and eats lunch each day with three or four students her age. The peers interact with her as a friend, helping her take part in the lunch conversation. The conversation is natural and the friends make sure that Lily asks and answers questions. They have also used the Lunch Bunch to make Lily more aware of how other teens dress and what they like to talk about – a great way for adolescents with AS to learn more about the hidden curriculum.

Social Skills Instruction

Youths with AS must be directly taught the skills they need to be successful socially. Direct instruction, acting lessons, and social stories are three ways in which they can learn social skills.

Direct instruction

Myles and Southwick (1999) offer the following direct instructional sequence to facilitate learning social skills: (a) rationale, (b) presentation, (c) modeling, (d) verification, (e) evaluation, and (f) generalization.

For instruction to be effective students with AS often need to understand the *rationale* – how or why concepts required for mastery are relevant. Thus, the rationale for a social skill should include (a) why the information is useful, (b) how the student can use the information, and (c) where it fits in with the knowledge the student already possesses. Presenting this information using a visual support will help the youth with AS understand what she is going to learn, the activities used to practice the skill, and the amount of time to be spent in social skills instruction. In other words, understanding the rationale for a given social skill helps "jump start" the learning process.

The *presentation* should be active and multimodal. That is, individuals with AS not only listen and/or view content, but respond to questions, are encouraged to share observations, and receive corrective feedback. Respect for the students' part-to-whole or whole-to-part learning style is also demonstrated. Since both types of learners may be present during a social skills lesson, the information must be presented using both formats in an effort to match each student's learning style. Direct instruction does *not* mean presenting a worksheet and telling the student to follow the directions.

During *modeling* the student is shown what to do. One common mistake must be avoided: We often tell students what *not* to do without providing the alternative – what they are supposed to do. First the student's attention must be directed to the model. The model should be presented frequently, with the context for its use clearly spelled out. We cannot infer that the student understands a specific concept or format just because it has been presented before. Anything merely implied will likely not be understood by the student.

> **Understanding the rationale for a given social skill helps "jump start" the learning process.**

Verification must occur throughout the lesson. That is, the teacher must closely monitor the student's understanding of what is being taught and his emotional state. Because students with AS often have a flat, even seemingly negative affect, it is difficult to tell when they are stressed as a result of not comprehending specific content. The teacher must work with the student to understand how he communicates emotional distress and meet his needs, as necessary, through additional instruction, modeling, or individual work sessions.

Following instruction, social skill acquisition requires *evaluation* from both the teacher and the student. A variety of methods should be employed to assess student understanding and use of the skill. For example, students should self-evaluate their skill performance and set goals for generalization and skill maintenance.

Finally, programming for *generalization* should be a part of every lesson through opportunities for students to use newly acquired social skills during the school day and in a variety of settings (i.e., physical education class, music). The student should also be observed in less structured settings, such as lunch and recess, to determine whether a given skill has truly been generalized. Assistance from parents is invaluable to ensure generalization. Specifically, they can set up and/or observe home- and community-based events in which the student is expected to use the skill.

Acting lessons

Many adults with AS recommend acting lessons to teach social skills. During these lessons, children learn to express – verbally and nonverbally – emotions in specific situations. They also learn to interpret others' emotions, feelings, and voices. Perhaps most important, actors engage in simulations and receive feedback about their performance (Myles & Southwick, 1999) in an environment that supports practice in a positive way.

Social stories

Carol Gray has created an effective way to provide both guidance and direction for responding to various social situations by using the strategy she calls social stories (Gray, 1995; Gray & Gerand, 1993; Swaggart et al., 1995). As defined by Gray, a *social story* is an individualized text or story that describes a specific social situation from the student's perspective. The description may include where and why the situation occurs, how others feel or react, or what prompts their feelings and reactions. After describing the social circumstance from the individual's perspective, the social story gives the student one or more options for what he can do in that particular situation. Gray's comprehensive guidelines for social story construction includes building in flexibility and using language appropriate to the student's cognitive level.

Tom, a 14-year-old with AS, was targeted by a group of boys as the object of their pranks. One of their pranks was to convince Tom to say curse words to other students and teachers. As expected, when Tom said the words only in the presence of his peers, they laughed. But, when he uttered them to both adults and students, they did not openly laugh. Tom did not understand why his peers laughed at certain times and not at others. He thought these boys were his friends and that their laughter was evidence of collegiality. He also did not understand why he was constantly getting in trouble. The social story presented in Table 4.6 was created specifically for Tom to provide him options for dealing with the hidden agenda item of knowing when and with whom to use certain words.

Social Skills Interpretation

Even with the most thorough social skills instruction, adolescents with AS encounter social situations they do not fully understand. As a result, they require someone who can interpret the encounter for them. Social skills interpreters act in a manner similar to that of language interpreters: Both translate unfamiliar content into a form that is more easily understood by the observer or listen-

---

Table 4.6
Social Story

Sometimes at school I hear kids say words that I haven't heard before. Kids may be saying these words to see my reaction or to get me into trouble. Sometimes kids are cruel.

When I hear new words, I have many choices. I can leave the situation, I can go ask the teacher for guidance, or I can answer with "I don't know what that means" and walk away.

If I choose to use these words, I need to understand that if the kids laugh, they may be laughing at me and not with me.

If my teacher hears me say these words, she may become upset and I may get in trouble. When I'm in trouble, I usually get upset.

When I hear a word that I don't understand, I need to find out what it means. Then I can make a good decision about using that word.

Created by Elisa Gagnon and Rebekah Heinrichs. Used with permission.

er. Little research exists on social skills instruction and social skills interpretation for individuals with AS. However, many anecdotal reports point to more success with interpretive than with instructional techniques. Several interpretation strategies help youths with AS understand their environment. These include: (a) cartooning; (b) social autopsies; (c) Situation-Options-Consequences-Choices-Strategies-Simulation (SOCCSS); and (d) sensory awareness.

Cartooning

Cartooning is a generic terms that has been used for years by speech-language pathologists to describe the drawing they do to explain situations, events, or language terms (such as idioms or metaphors) to their clients. Cartooning strategies have been refined by Arwood and Brown (1999) in their book, *A Guide to Cartooning and Flowcharting: See the Ideas.* They call the cartoon a "form of visual language" and "story telling in picture form" (p. 1). The cartoon is used to:

• explain and change behavior
• improve social skills
• manage time
• improve academic skills
• help students clarify or refine their ideas

Arwood and Brown offer guidelines for how to draw cartoons, including (a) using connected frames to illustrate sequence, (b) grounding the characters within the cartoon so that there is no air between the person and the ground, and (c) making the drawn ideas move in one direction only. Figure 4.5 shows an example of a cartoon for social change – *Mark wants to make friends, but he stands too close to other students.*

Also using cartoons, Gray (1994) introduced comic strip conversations to illustrate and interpret social situations and to provide support to "students who struggle to comprehend the quick exchange of information which occurs in a conversation" (p. 1). According to Gray, "Comic strip conversations regard the thoughts and feelings of others as holding equal importance to spoken words and actions in an interaction" (p. 2). They promote social understanding by incorporating simple figures and other symbols in a comic strip format. Speech, conversation bubble symbols, and color

From *A Guide to Cartooning and Flowcharting* (p. 3), by Ellyn Lucas Arwood, Ed.D., CCC-SLP, and Mabel M. Brown, M. A., 1999. Apricot, Inc., P.O. Box, 18191, Portland, OR 97218; www.spiritone.com/~apricot. Used with permission.

Figure 4.5. *Sample cartoon.*

are used to help the individual with AS see and analyze a conversation. Gray (1994) has also designed a conversation symbols dictionary, which illustrates listening, interrupting, talking, using loud or quiet words, or thinking. In addition, she has created a color chart that associates emotions with color. For example, green represents good ideas, being happy or acting friendly; red symbolizes bad ideas, teasing, anger, or acting in an unfriendly manner; and yellow denotes feeling frightened.

Social autopsies

The social autopsy is an innovative strategy developed by Lavoie (Bieber, 1994) to help students with social problems understand social mistakes. Simply stated, the social autopsy is a vehicle for analyzing a social skills problem. Following a social error, the student who committed the error works with an adult to (a) identify the error, (b) determine who was harmed by the error, (c) decide how to correct the error, and (d) develop a plan so that the error does not occur again.

A social skills autopsy is not a punishment. Rather, it is a supportive and constructive problem-solving strategy. According to Lavoie (cited in Bieber, 1994), "The autopsy process is particularly effective in enabling the child to see the cause/effect relationship between his social behavior and the reactions of others in his environment" (p. 11). Lavoie posits that the success of the strategy lies in its structure of practice, immediate feedback, and positive reinforcement. Every adult with whom the student with AS has regular contact, such as parents, bus drivers, teachers, custodians, and cafeteria workers, should know how to do a social skills autopsy fostering skill acquisition and generalization. Figure 4.6 provides a worksheet that can be used to structure social autopsies.

Situation-Options-Consequences-Choices-Strategies-Simulation (SOCCSS)

Jan Roosa (personal communication, 1995) developed the Situation-Options-Consequences-Choices-Strategies-Simulation (SOCCSS) strategy to help students with social disabilities understand social situations and develop problem-solving skills by putting social and behavioral issues into a sequential form. This teacher-directed strategy helps students understand cause and effect and realize that they can influence the outcome of many situations by the decisions they make. The strategy can be used one on one with a student or can take place as a group activity, depending on the situation and students' needs. SOCCSS contains the following six steps.

SITUATION: After a social problem occurs, the teacher helps the student to identify who, what, when, where, and why. Who was involved in the situation? What actually happened? When did it

Social Autopsies Worksheet

What happened? _____

_____

_____

_____

What was the social error?	Who was hurt by the social error?

What should be done to correct the error? _____

_____

_____

_____

What could be done next time? _____

_____

_____

_____

_____

_____

_____

_____

_____

Figure 4.6. *Social autopsies worksheet.*

happen? Where did the problem occur? Why did it happen? The goal is to encourage the student to relate these variables independently. However, at first the teacher assumes an active role in prompting and identifying, when necessary, the answers to these questions.

OPTIONS: The teacher and student brainstorm several behavioral options the student could have chosen. Brainstorming means that the teacher accepts and records all student responses without evaluating them. Initially, the teacher usually has to encourage the student to identify more than one thing he could have done or said differently.

CONSEQUENCES: For each behavior option generated, a consequence is listed. The teacher asks the student, "So what would happen if you … (name the option)?" Some options may have more than one consequence. It is often hard for students with AS to generate consequences because of their difficulty determining cause-and-effect relationships. Role-play at this stage can serve as a prompt in identifying the consequence.

CHOICES: Options and consequences are prioritized using a numerical sequence or a yes/no response. Following prioritization, the student is prompted to select the option that she thinks (a) she will be able to do and (b) will most likely get her what she wants or needs.

STRATEGIES: The next step involves developing a plan to carry out the option if the situation occurs. Although the teacher and youth collaborate on the stages of the plan, the student should generate the plan. This is important because the student needs to feel that he has been the decision maker and is responsible for the plan.

SIMULATION: Practice is the fifth stage in SOCCSS. Roosa has defined this practice in a variety of ways: (a) using imagery, (b) talking with another about the plan, (c) writing down the plan, or (d) role-playing. The student ends up evaluating his impressions of the simulation. Did the simulation activity give him the skills and confidence to carry out the plan? If the answer is "no," additional simulation must take place.

Although designed as interpretive, this strategy can also be used as an instructional strategy. Teachers can identify problems students are likely to encounter and address them using SOCCSS so that students have a plan prior to a situation occurring (Myles & Simpson, 1998, 2001; Myles & Southwick, 1999).

Figure 4.7 provides a worksheet that can be used to facilitate the SOCCSS process.

Sensory awareness

All the information we receive from the environment comes through our sensory system. Thus, the senses of taste, smell, sight, sound, touch, movement, gravity force, and balance impact learning (Ayres, 1979). Many individuals with AS have sensory problems and therefore require direct assistance in this area (Myles et al., 2000). Several programs, including those mentioned below, appear effective in meeting the sensory needs of children and youth with AS.

How Does Your Engine Run: The Alert Program for Self-Regulation (Williams & Shellenberger, 1996) helps individuals recognize their sensory issues, particularly as they relate to arousal or awareness. This self-empowering program teaches adolescents to change their level of alertness in response to academic or social demands.

The Tool Chest for Teachers, Parents, and Students (Henry Occupational Therapy Services, 1998) emphasizes behavior as a means of communication and helps adult users to develop sensory strategies that prevent behavior problems. Two videotapes supplement the program by demonstrating important strategies.

Building Bridges Through Sensory Integration (Yak et al., 1998) discusses the role of occupational therapy and sensory integration specifically for persons with autism or other pervasive developmental disorders. User-friendly checklists identify sensory issues that are addressed through a series of activities provided in the curriculum.

Asperger Syndrome and Sensory Issues: Practical Solutions for Making Sense of the World (Myles et al., 2000) is the only book that specifically addresses the sensory problems experienced by individuals with AS. The book overviews the impact of sensory integration dysfunction on the academic, social, and behavior domains. In addition, it contains instruments to assess social issues and discusses strategies for addressing these concerns for effective social and academic functioning.

SOCCSS
Situation–Options–Consequences–Choices–Strategies–Simulation

Situation

Who _____

What _____

When _____

Why _____

Options	Consequences	Choices

Strategy – Plan of Action

Figure 4.7. *SOCCSS worksheet.*

SOCCSS
Situation–Options–Consequences–Choices–Strategies–Simulation

Simulation		Select One
1. Find a quiet place, sit back and imagine how your Situation would work (or not work) based on the various Options and Consequences.		
2. Talk with a peer, staff, or other person about your plan of action.		
3. Write down on paper what may happen in your Situation based on your Options and Consequences.		
4. Practice your Options with one or more people using behavior rehearsal. Start simple and easy for learning. Only make it difficult to test the learning.		
5. _____		

Simulation Outcomes

Followup

Figure 4.7. (continued)

Stabilization

As previously mentioned, adolescents with AS experience stress, anxiety and depression that has been linked to difficulties in adapting to change, predicting what will happen next, understanding the social interactions and intentions of others, and so forth. When teens have difficulty adapting to their environment, they may begin a "downward spiral" into tantrums, rage, and meltdowns. When this cycle begins, the priority must be to stabilize them. "Stabilization" refers to the process of creating an environment that assists the individual in becoming more stable and therefore functioning better.

Short-Term Interventions

Stabilization strategies may be required because of short- or long-term events. If an adolescent experiences several changes or disappointments within a short period of time, she may become less stable or more vulnerable to a tantrum, rage, or meltdown. To become more stable, in this situation, the teen needs the environment adapted. The adaptations are often minor and may include antiseptic bouncing, support from routine, reassurance, proximity control, "just walk and don't talk" or home base.[4]

For example, when Roberto came into the cafeteria he saw that the tables were not in their usual place; they were moved to the far side of the room. He got into the lunch line and found that the cafeteria was out of pizza, the food he ate almost every day. Roberto chose a hotdog instead. Mr. Smith, the assistant principal, monitors Roberto's lunch period and knows him well. He noticed that two of Roberto's peers who have teased him in the past sat down at his table. As a result, he walked over to Roberto's table frequently during the lunch period, checking to make sure that Roberto was okay, and listening to gain a sense of the peer interactions. Mr. Smith also made it a point to ask Roberto about recent political debates because that is one of Roberto's special interests. In addition, when Roberto

---

[4] Refer to Myles, B. S., & Southwick, J. (1999). *Asperger Syndrome and difficult moments: Practical solutions for tantrums, rage, and meltdowns.* Shawnee Mission, KS: AAPC.

finished eating, Mr. Smith gave him a job to do – taking a note to the office – that enabled him to leave the lunchroom area.

In this instance, Roberto experienced three minor stressors (rearrangement of the lunchroom, no pizza, and exposure to peers with whom he had problems). Mr. Smith reacted to the situation by making sure that Roberto was safe from teasing by focusing on one of his favorite topics (political debates) and asking Roberto to take a note to the office, thereby giving him an opportunity to leave the cafeteria (antiseptic bouncing).

Long-Term Intervention

Stabilization for individuals who have had long-term problems is different. The longer the student has been in a downward spiral, the more difficult it is to reverse the trend. Meghan is repeating the ninth grade in a general education setting. Her teachers report that she seems withdrawn and depressed and is producing no work. This was true last year as well. Even when the teacher prompts her to produce work, Meghan says she can't or puts her head down on her desk and sleeps. Her behavioral program consists of a token economy system that is tallied weekly. Frequently Meghan does not earn enough tokens for a reward. When an outside consultant suggested that the curriculum needed further adaptation around Meghan's interests, staff emphasized that she needed to participate in the regular curriculum since she is on the standard diploma track.

Changing Meghan's situation will require a significant cognitive shift on the part of the school team serving her. Once a student has "shut down," she is incapable of coping with many typical school demands. It does not matter that the student has an average or above-average IQ. That, in and of itself, does not mean that the student is in an emotional state that allows her to produce what the environment is demanding. It is essential that the school team (including parents) recognize the fragile emotional state of the student with AS and adapt the environment to meet her needs.

Meghan was eventually moved to a resource room setting where a teacher could work with her one on one. Curricular demands were modified drastically. All instruction focused around her special interest, electromagnetism, and assignments contained tasks that

Meghan had previously mastered. The daily schedule was structured and consistent. Visual supports were used to help Meghan keep track of her day. Stressors, such as tests and handwriting, were removed. Emphasis was placed on motivating Meghan to learn, increasing her self-esteem, and making her feel safe and comfortable. Her parents, deciding that therapy would be beneficial, found a therapist who understood AS. The therapist bonded with Meghan and helped her develop better self-esteem and a sense of trust toward her teachers and parents. As Meghan's emotional state began to improve, her teacher and therapist worked on helping Meghan recognize her own indicators of stress and seeking assistance when needed. Six months later, Meghan was ready to gradually transition back into general education. Her school team, deciding to move her into one class at a time, helped her to transition into science first – an area of strength and motivation to Meghan.

Five Steps to Help Stabilize a Student with AS

The following five steps can help students who require stabilization:

1. *Gather information from a number of sources to assess the student's emotional state.* Students with AS require continuous monitoring of their emotional status. Often teachers and parents miss the signs that signal the beginning of a crisis. This is due, in part, to the communication deficits of students with AS. That is, students with AS are often ineffective at recognizing in themselves and subsequently conveying anxiety, frustration, anger, or depression until these emotions reach crisis proportions. Therefore, educators and parents must become skilled at recognizing the initial behavioral signs of stress and anxiety. Melinda's teachers and parents know that when she starts to pace back and forth, she is anxious. Sam runs his hand through his hair when he encounters too much stress. Min begins to rock back and forth when he experiences difficulty.

A second indicator of declining emotional status includes any deterioration in academic, social or behavior functioning at school or home. It is important to keep in mind that academic decline includes a student with AS who usually gets an "A" in science and now is getting a "C."

It is common for schools to report that the student is doing fine during the school day (no behavioral outbursts, good attention to task, appropriate social skills), whereas parents report that the adolescent falls apart at home (uncontrollable tantrums, verbal outbursts, aggression against siblings) (Myles & Southwick, 1999). This type of behavior at home signals that stressors may exist in school and/or at home.

2. *Determine the stressors that exist in the environment.* Examine the environment using the strategies outlined in Chapter 3. It is important to determine whether any changes have occurred at school or home that might have caused or contributed to the downward spiral. For example:

- Has the student had to cope with a substitute teacher?
- Has the regular schedule been interrupted (i.e., assemblies, testing)?
- Does the student have a long-term assignment to do with no idea about how to begin?
- Has the structure in specific classes been changed (from individual work to cooperative groups)?
- Has the adolescent been exposed to increased incidents of teasing and/or bullying?
- Has the student reported difficulties in working with a particular student?
- Has increased emphasis been placed on getting good grades?

Parents may want to consider whether there have been any significant changes in the home. For example, when Susan's brother, Tim, began to excel at gymnastics, Susan had to accompany Tim and her mother twice a week to practice. Although Susan could do her homework at the gym, it was not the same as being at home. In addition, by going to the gym she missed her favorite after-school television show. Both of these events made her upset and stressed.

If no changes have occurred at home, parents may want to consider a checkup with their physician to determine whether the adolescent is ill. If neither of these seems to be contributing factors, it is usually necessary to look closely at the school environment.

3. *Decrease the stressors by modifying the requirements for disliked and/or difficult tasks and temporarily eliminating any emphasis on teaching new skills.* To stabilize the school environment and stop the

escalating crisis, we must increase supports immediately and reduce stressors. School personnel should "try to identify – *in advance* – specific situations that may routinely lead to inflexible-explosive episodes" (Green, 1998, p. 274).

If the difficulty experienced in one area is of considerable magnitude or if the student is experiencing difficulty in a number of areas, it is important that interventions be implemented on multiple levels concurrently. When supports are increased tenfold, the student is more likely to bounce back than if supports are increased one by one over several weeks or months. Thus, it is important for the adolescent to receive some respite from stressors. For example, if a major stressor for the student is coping with the long-term substitute language arts teacher, the school team (including the parents) may decide that the student can receive language arts instruction in a resource room. In addition, the language arts requirements may be modified for the next long-term assignment.

When the student is in a fragile emotional state, school personnel and parents must recognize the necessity of temporarily lowering their expectations. The adolescent may need to know how to write essays in the future when she attends college, but that does not mean that in a crisis state she must practice writing every day. The more fragile the emotional state, the more crucial it is that the stressors be alleviated.

While reducing stressors, it may be important at the same time to provide more opportunities for the student with AS to engage in activities of high interest and/or activities that emphasize the student's strengths. Mohammed derives considerable self-esteem from the fact that many teachers call on him to assist with various computer problems. When Mohammed began having meltdowns during PE, a variety of interventions were put in place. When these were not successful, the school team decided to waive the PE requirement and build additional computer technical assistance opportunities into Mohammed's daily schedule.

4. *Make the environment more predictable and increase the use of home base.* The student's many environments should be reanalyzed to ensure a high level of consistency and to make sure that the teen knows the routine for each class. Priming may need to be used more often. In addition, the student may need scheduled home base peri-

ods that occur both prior to and following a class that is especially difficult. For example, Jerry's homeroom teacher has noticed that he is often on edge when he arrives at school. Knowing his interest in drawing cartoon figures, his homeroom teacher allows Jerry to come to the classroom as soon as his bus arrives, thereby giving him 15 to 20 minutes to draw and getting himself ready to face the school day.

5. *Balance stressors and learning.* As the youth becomes more stable, it is possible to gradually increase the demands. The key to success is to continually monitor the student's emotional status and maintain supports. As we increase demands, careful assessment must determine whether the individual has the skill(s) to perform the increased demands. If not, a plan must be developed to teach the skills. For some adolescents, instruction should occur in a structured classroom-type setting. Others may benefit from "planned moments of instruction," that is, providing a brief explanation or coaching when a social error happens. However, care should be taken that this instruction is not a stressor in itself.

> **... the key to success is to continually monitor the student's emotional status and maintain supports.**

Jerry's school created a social skills group just for him. But after a while, his teachers noticed that he began to talk about the group a day or two before it was scheduled. In addition, they reported an increase in Jerry's identified anxiety behaviors (humming, rubbing his eyes, and repeated questioning) the day before the group was to meet. Noting his agitation, Jerry's parents and school team decided that he would benefit more from embedded instruction than continued participation in the social skills group.

Frequently, insight-oriented therapy or a talk session with a counselor or therapist is recommended for the youth with AS. For some individuals, however, this type of intervention increases stress and anxiety rather than providing meaningful assistance. When the goal is stabilization, it is helpful to assess the youth's response to discussions about feelings as well as his response to discussions about past upsetting events and plan any therapy accordingly.

For others, therapy can be an essential part of the overall intervention plan. It is important that the teen with AS be instructed in the rules of therapy such as open, honest communication, as this can be considered part of the hidden curriculum. Otherwise, it is possible that the adolescent will sit through therapy sessions giving the answers the therapist wants rather than sharing her true feelings.

As mentioned, therapy is not the only component required for recovery. Parents and professionals need to realize that a few hours of therapy will not compensate for a lack of support throughout the day. It is essential that the school team identify contributing factors and devise comprehensive strategies to turn the situation around for the adolescent with AS.

Summary

Adolescents with AS need multifaceted supports to ensure school success. Supports matching student needs must be individualized, structured, flexible, and predictable. It is also important that the supports are positively oriented rather than deficit-driven. That is, they must focus on students' talents and on effecting changes that will have a meaningful outcome for the youth in school, home, and community. Throughout the teen years, students should gradually be taught to assume responsibility for requesting and monitoring needed accommodations in preparation for adulthood where they will ultimately be responsible for structuring their own environment for success.

CHAPTER 5

Transition Planning for the Student with Asperger Syndrome

Authored with Jennifer Stella, University of Miami

As we have mentioned repeatedly in this book, the transition to middle and high school is difficult for most students, but will likely have more stressful and long-lasting effects on the student with AS than on the typical student. Most typical students need some support, at least temporarily, to transition successfully to the secondary level, such as carrying their new schedule around with them for the first week or getting to school early to reach their locker in time to get ready. Most of these students have needed little, if any support, during their elementary school years.

But the situation is different for many students with AS. Given their continuing challenges combined with the added demands of middle and high school, and the hormonal changes of puberty, they will likely need significantly more supports during the transition to middle and high school (Adreon & Stella, 2001).

To make the experience as positive as possible, parents and teachers must be proactive in transition planning. Transition must not be thought of as a one-shot deal. Instead, it should be viewed as an ongoing process that addresses the changing academic, social, emotional, and physical needs of the student.

Transition planning must first identify all needed supports and then make sure they are ready to be implemented before school begins in the fall. Given the potential for aggravating the often tenuous success of youths with AS during the transition to middle and high school, this chapter takes a step-by-step look at the components of effective transition planning. So many of the stressors that characterize this period of all students' lives are particularly anxiety-provoking for students with AS. Hence parents and educators must do everything in their power to work together to maximize the students' academic, social, and behavioral development. Specifically, we will look at program/school options to be considered and training and orientation for both teachers and students. A centerpiece of the chapter is a comprehensive checklist designed to help ensure that all necessary steps are in place for a smooth transition. This checklist correlates with major supports and issues discussed in Chapter 4.

Conducting and/or Reviewing Assessments

Meaningful assessment records can serve as initial guides to the transition planning process. As stated in Chapter 3, this includes (a) diagnostic assessment (if this has not been previously completed); (b) curriculum-based assessment of academic strengths and concerns; (c) formal and informal measures of sensory, social, and language skills; and (d) functional assessment of behaviors and perceptions. These assessments provide the groundwork for an appropriate education for the adolescent with AS.

Selecting the Appropriate School Environment

Depending on the community in which the student lives, the size of the school district, and other family and community factors, several placement options are usually available and should be considered as future programming is planned. Because students will AS typically experience increasing difficulties as they move into more complex environments, it is strongly recommended that possible environments be carefully analyzed early in the year prior to the transition.

Families and school personnel should take into serious consideration the impressions and opinions of the individual with AS when selecting a program to ensure that the youth buys into the program and therefore will be more likely to do well. If possible, it is important to explore several options and help the adolescent with AS see a range of options. Here we will briefly review the main characteristics of public, magnet, and private schools, as well as discuss the recent reemergence of homeschooling.

In addition to the planning steps and decisions outlined in the preceding chapters, successful transition and continued maximum student performance depend on proper implementation of the various modifications deemed necessary for a given student. These were discussed in detail in Chapter 4 under the major headings of Academic Modifications, Modifications for Unstructured and Less Structured Times of the School Day, Environmental Supports, and Social Supports. Their inclusion in the Transition Checklist (see Figure 5.1) underscores their importance to the overall academic and behavioral/emotional success of the student with AS.

Public schools

Most public school districts adhere to a set feeder pattern that specifies the home school a student will move to as a next environment. Attending the home school allows the student to be with youths who live in the same general area. Therefore, neighborhood school attendance may provide more opportunities to foster social relationships beyond the school setting. Another reason why many families opt for their neighborhood school is that it usually makes transportation for their child less complicated and shorter – whether they choose to drive themselves or use the district bus system.

As part of their decision on whether to send their son or daughter to the local public school, some families check out the reputation of the administration at various schools to assess: (a) the school administration's reputation regarding discipline policies; (b) attitudes toward students with special needs; (c) implications for dealing with the "challenging behaviors" of many students with AS; and (d) types of responses and supports the administration provides in dealing with teasing and bullying.

If the public school option seems best, other issues must be considered jointly with school staff. These include questions such as: Should the youth be placed in general education with paraprofessional support? Would resource room placement with some general education classes be more appropriate? Or does a self-contained program that provides an age- and grade-appropriate curriculum seem the best option?

Recent research suggests that the average IQ of individuals with AS is about 100. However, the percentage of students with AS who have a superior or very superior IQ exceeds that of the general population (Barnhill et al., 2000). Therefore, a greater than average number of youth with AS meet school eligibility for gifted educational programs. Some school districts offer full- or part-time gifted pullout programs at the middle and high school level. In other schools, qualifying students filter into advanced placement courses.

Many students with AS who have above-average IQs derive a significant portion of their self-esteem from their acceptance into gifted and advanced programs, making it particularly important to ensure they are accommodated in such programs as widely as possible. In addition, many students with AS, particularly those with pedantic language, may be better understood by peers in these programs. However, despite these benefits, too frequently students with AS in gifted programs encounter limited flexibility in terms of the quantity of work required and the amount of curriculum modifications provided. When this occurs, they are generally not successful. For these reasons, the specifics of a given program need to be explored ahead of time to ensure a good fit.

Magnet schools

Due to the highly specialized interests of many students with AS in such subjects as general science, engineering, computer technology, animal science, and the arts, participation in magnet specialty programs is often a viable option. In addition to intensive instruction in areas of special interest, these programs often attract motivated teachers who are highly specialized and therefore are better able to provide stimulating and challenging learning experiences. Further, the student with AS often fares better socially in an academic program that includes students who share similar interests. Finally, many magnet schools are smaller than typical middle or high schools, which is an added benefit for students with AS.

When considering magnet school attendance careful planning is particularly critical for several reasons. First, in some districts, the deadline for applying to specialty programs is as early as January of the prior year. Further, these programs often have requirements based on standardized testing scores, academic grades, and behavior.

Also, the majority of these programs are required to maintain the ethnic/racial balance of the community at large, which may influence the chances of a given student being accepted. In some communities, programs are subject to a lottery, making admission even more random.

Another consideration relates to transportation. Many specialty programs are located a considerable distance from the student's home, requiring the use of school transportation. The pros and cons of a particular student riding the bus should be considered in the early planning stages. One of the advantages of magnet buses for many students with AS is that they may have interests in common with their fellow students and have opportunities to share them on the ride to and from school. This has important implications for social skills development and establishing friendships beyond school.

Private schools

Some families explore private school options for their children with AS. Many private schools are regarded as prestigious preparatory schools and may have long waiting lists. Typically, these schools do not provide accommodations for students with special needs. Currently, few private schools are specifically designed to serve individuals with AS in middle and high school.

However, a number of private schools are truly interested in serving students with special needs. The curriculum in many of these programs, particularly those designed for students with learning disabilities, adapt or modify the academic demands that are frequently challenging for students with AS. These include (a) taking notes, (b) keeping track of homework assignments, (c) breaking down long-term projects into manageable steps and completing them following a timetable, (d) reducing or eliminating homework, and (e) reducing writing demands. In many instances, these programs are not designed to meet the needs of students who are accelerated in some academic areas, however.

One of the primary reasons why families choose private schools is the smaller class size and greater opportunities for individual attention that are often offered. Some feel that a private school provides a more "sheltered" environment for a child who may be socially immature and exhibits poor social judgment.

Many parents of children with AS choose to "not tell" the school about their child's diagnosis as they have heard that a particular school will not accept students with AS. While we understand the temptation to withhold this information, parents potentially harm their son's or daughter's chances of success and academic and· social/emotional adjustment by minimizing the child's difficulties. In downplaying these issues, many parents are "thankful" that their child is allowed to attend a particular school. Others live in constant fear that their child will be asked to leave the school because he or she is "not adjusting" or is exhibiting too many "behavioral challenges." In most instances, a private school is under little obligation to adapt its program to meet the needs of a particular student.

Some families of adolescents with AS change from one private school to another over several years in the hope of finding the right program for their child. Every year, they make a change because the program is not "working," only to find another school that will accept the student but that ends up not "working" either. The adolescent who is exposed to this "school hopping" almost never receives needed curricular and social modifications, views school negatively, and has a high stress level.

Homeschooling

Some parents have decided that the homeschooling option best matches their teen's needs. This alternative provides parents greater control over social interactions and curricula than is possible in a traditional school setting. Despite the apparent advantages associated with a home-based education, this decision must be made very carefully. Although homeschooling networks provide curricula and educational resources to parents who serve as their child's teacher, parents must be content area experts or know how to access such individuals, recruit ancillary personnel (such as speech-language pathologists and occupational therapists) to meet their youth's individual needs, as well as provide opportunities for varied social interactions.

The Transition Planning Meeting

Once the school has been selected – whether public or private – the next step in ensuring a successful transition is to hold a transition planning meeting. Whenever possible, it is important that personnel is in attendance from both the school being transitioned "from" and the school being transitioned "to" to ensure continuing communication and support (Adreon & Stella, 2001).

During the meeting all participants should focus on identifying supports the student needs to survive the first weeks of school and determining how to implement them. It is also important to set up a schedule for future meetings and any training that is deemed necessary. As discussed below, sound transition planning includes teacher training as well as student orientation. Depending on the student's needs and the nature of the program being transitioned into, the planning meeting may need to be scheduled as early as the spring before the transition in order to allow sufficient planning time. Figure 5.1 overviews the agenda for the transition planning meeting.

> **It is important that personnel is in attendance from both the school being transitioned "from" and the school being transitioned "to."**

Training for School Personnel

When the best placement/school was selected for the student with AS, a major consideration should have been to ensure that the faculty and staff understand AS and how this disorder affects the student's behavioral and academic performance. However, even if this condition has been satisfied initially, it may still be necessary to check that staff understand how to implement the various modifications/adaptations and strategies that were determined for the student during the transition planning meeting. If additional training is deemed necessary, it should take place before the start of the new school year and, as far as possible, before the student's orientation process so the teachers are familiar with the student's behaviors and needs before meeting her for the first time. Guidelines for staff training and orientation appear in Figure 5.1.

Transition Checklist:

Creating a Successful Middle and High School Experience for Youth with Asperger Syndrome
PREPLANNING

Conducting or Reviewing Assessments
- ❏ Ensure that all staff who will be working with the youth understand the student's strengths and concerns.

Choosing Next Environment
- ❏ Visit different types of programs or programs at different schools to determine appropriate placement options.

Transition Planning Meeting
- ❏ Create the student's schedule. Careful attention should be paid to choosing specials and creating opportunities for "downtime" where the student can engage in preferred activities to decrease anxiety levels.
- ❏ Create, review, and/or revise the IEP or 504 Plan to ensure that all necessary adaptations and modifications are included (i.e., homework, class work, lunch, physical education, before-school activities).
- ❏ Identify a teacher or administrator who will serve as the primary school contact for the parent to discuss any problems or changes that may occur.
- ❏ Identify a team of individuals at the school who will serve as "safe persons."
- ❏ Schedule dates and content of training sessions for school personnel. Plan to complete all training before the first day of school – if possible, before student orientation.
- ❏ Plan an orientation schedule for the student. Many schools provide a general orientation for all students transitioning to middle school in the spring of the final year of elementary school. Students with AS need a more extensive orientation process than typical students. Suggestions for orientation activities are provided under Student Orientation. The majority of the orientation activities may be conducted during the week before the start of the school year.

Training for School Personnel
- ❏ Conduct a general orientation for all personnel at the school.

This training session should:
- ❏ Overview the characteristics of individuals with AS
- ❏ Provide information on the specific behavioral, academic, and emotional concerns of the student
- ❏ Include all teachers, counselors, administrators, office staff, cafeteria workers, security, etc., who will have contact with the student
- ❏ Provide training on how to implement the strategies determined during the transition planning meeting and/or included in the student's IEP or 504

Figure 5.1. *Transition checklist.*

Plan. All teachers, counselors, and administrators in contact with the student should be present.

This training session should include information on:

❑ The specific, step-by-step procedure the student can use to seek out the safe person and get to home base

❑ The procedure to be followed for behavioral problems

❑ The procedure for ensuring that homework assignments are recorded and that required materials are brought home

❑ How to implement all academic modifications, accommodations, and supports

❑ Any other needs or issues that require discussion

Student Orientation

❑ Provide a walk-through of the student's daily schedule. In schools where the schedule changes from day to day, the student should have the opportunity to practice all possible schedules. If applicable, student "buddies" should be available to walk through the schedule with the student with AS.

The following are suggestions for the walk-through:

❑ Provide visual/written class schedule(s) for the student.

❑ Videotape a walk-through school schedule for the student to review at home.

❑ Practice route(s) from various classes to the bathroom, counselor's office, home base, etc.

❑ Meet all teachers and relevant personnel.

❑ Provide the student with pictures and names of all teachers in advance of the orientation.

❑ Provide the student with pictures and names of all support personnel, such as safe person, counselors, special education coordinators, assistant principals and principal, in advance of the orientation.

❑ Provide the student with pictures and names of all additional personnel, such as cafeteria workers, school nurse, etc.

❑ Provide the student with pictures and names of student "buddies."

❑ Show the student where her assigned seat in each classroom will be.

❑ Obtain information about school routines and rules (i.e., lunch, going to bathroom, before/after school, transportation).

❑ Practice routines such as finding homeroom from the bus stop, opening locker, going through the cafeteria line, etc.

❑ Provide instruction on the procedure for seeking out the safe person and home base.

❑ Practice use of transition to home base through role-play.

ACADEMIC MODIFICATIONS

Priming

❑ Determine whether priming will help meet the student's need for predictability.

Figure 5.1. *(continued)*

❑ Analyze student needs and classroom demands to determine which classes will require priming.
❑ Identify who will prime.
❑ Designate whether priming will use actual or similar materials.
❑ Determine where and when priming will occur.

Classroom Assignments

❑ Determine the student's needs concerning assignments.
❑ Provide the student with extra time to complete assignments.
❑ Shorten the length of assignments.
❑ Reduce the number of assignments.
❑ Break assignments into smaller segments.
❑ Provide samples/models of completed assignments and/or a list of specific criteria for successful completion.
❑ Allow the student to use the computer for schoolwork and/or homework.
❑ Allow the student to demonstrate mastery of concepts through alternate means (dictate essays, oral tests, etc.).

Notetaking

❑ Indicate the type of notetaking supports needed by the student.
❑ Provide a complete outline.
❑ Give student a skeletal outline.
❑ Identify a peer who can take notes for the student.
❑ Allow student to use outlining software.

Graphic Organizers

❑ Determine whether graphic organizers are needed to facilitate skill acquisition and maintenance.
❑ Specify which type of graphic organizers will be needed:
  ❑ Hierarchical
  ❑ Conceptual
  ❑ Sequential
  ❑ Cyclical
  ❑ Other
❑ Determine who will construct and provide organizer to student:
  ❑ Teacher
  ❑ Peer
  ❑ Student with template
  ❑ Student with outlining software

Enrichment

❑ Determine the type of enrichment needed:
  ❑ Specify how the enrichment area will be identified.
  ❑ Determine when and how enrichment will be provided.
  ❑ Decide whether a learning contract with specified working conditions is needed.

Figure 5.1. *(continued)*

Homework

❑ Identify which class subjects will include homework responsibilities.
❑ Determine homework modifications:
    ❑ Present homework assignments visually (on board, etc.) in addition to orally.
    ❑ Provide the student with a homework sheet or planner.
    ❑ Provide peer or teacher assistance in recording homework assignments.
    ❑ Provide student with the assignment in written format.
    ❑ Reduce the amount of homework.
    ❑ Provide a study hall period to allow the student time to complete homework at school.
❑ Identify home strategy for completing homework:
    ❑ Designate place and time for homework completion.
    ❑ Define organization to get homework back to school.
    ❑ Name contact if additional clarification on homework is needed.

MODIFICATIONS FOR UNSTRUCTURED OR LESS STRUCTURED TIMES

Transportation/Bus

❑ Identify who will teach the student the bus routine.
❑ Determine who will provide assistance for the student when the bus arrives at school, particularly on the first day. Have a peer or school staff greet the student at the bus and accompany him to the bus at the end of the day.
❑ Determine how long assistance will be needed in getting to and from the bus throughout the school year.
❑ Identify the peer or school personnel to be assigned to assist the student in this process, including backups.
❑ Provide a pickup or dropoff closer to the student's house.
❑ Provide adult supervision at the bus stop.
❑ Provide a peer "buddy" from the student's neighborhood to wait with the student at the bus stop and sit with her on the bus.
❑ Provide preferential seating on the bus. This may include seating the student in close proximity to the driver or allowing her to sit in her own seat/row.
❑ Provide a monitor or aide on the bus.
❑ Provide a special bus.

Physical Education

❑ Consider whether to exempt the student from physical education and, if so, substitute another special or a study hall. This is particularly important if poor motor skills have led to teasing or rejection by peers.
❑ Assign the student a specific role for PE such as score keeper, equipment manager, etc. This allows him to participate in PE, but minimizes the motor and social demands of playing a sport.
❑ Assign teams rather than allow students to choose teams themselves.

Figure 5.1. *(continued)*

❏ Have school personnel monitor, at least twice weekly, the student's perceptions of the PE period by asking her how she feels it is going.
❏ Help the student problem-solve difficulties.

Lunch

❏ Have school personnel available during the first week of school to assist the student in navigating the cafeteria line, finding a place to sit, and engaging in an appropriate activity once he has finished eating.
❏ Help the student identify school personnel whom she can approach during the lunch period when encountering problems.
❏ Have school personnel closely monitor the student's interactions with peers and intervene when problems occur.
❏ Have school personnel closely monitor the student and intervene when she becomes stressed and overwhelmed or begins to experience sensory overload.
❏ Have school personnel monitor, at least twice weekly, the student's perceptions of the lunch period by asking the student how he/she feels it is going.
❏ Help the student problem-solve any difficulties.
❏ Provide assigned seating with a preferred friend, away from problem peers and/or near adult supervision.
❏ Provide peer "buddy/buddies" during lunchtime.
❏ Allow the student to leave the cafeteria once he has finished eating to engage in a calming or preferred activity (e.g., go to media center, computer lab).
❏ Allow the student to eat lunch in an alternative location if necessary (e.g., counselor's office, media center).

Changing Classes

❏ Provide peer or teacher assistance (particularly during the first week of school) to help the student manage the crowded hallways, open locker, locate the proper materials, and find the correct classroom.
❏ Provide a peer "buddy" to accompany the student during class changes if he continues to experience difficulty during this time. This "buddy" might assist the student with organizational issues, protect against teasing/bullying by other students, and help promote positive social interactions.
❏ Provide the student with additional time for class changes.
❏ Allow alternate passing time when the hallways are free from other students. For example, the student might change classes before or after the general transition period.

Changes in Routine

❏ Specify whether the student needs to be informed of any changes in typical classroom procedures (assemblies, fire drills, guest speakers, seating changes, substitute teacher).

Figure 5.1. *(continued)*

❑ Determine what additional supports the student needs when changes occur.

Before and After School

❑ Identify when the student should arrive at school.
❑ Determine whether a specific room will be used during this time.
❑ Identify peers to support the student at this time.
❑ Provide structured activities.

ENVIRONMENTAL SUPPORTS

Preferential Seating

❑ Determine if preferential seating is necessary:
  ❑ Identify location.
  ❑ Identify peers who can support student.

Organizational Strategies

❑ Determine the student's needs concerning organization of papers and materials.
❑ Provide assistance in organizing the backpack, locker, and/or desk and teach the student to do so independently.
❑ Teach the student to use timelines.
❑ Instruct the student on how to develop a to-do list.

Home Base

❑ Identify when home base will be used:
  ❑ Before school or early morning
  ❑ Following specific classes
  ❑ At the end of the day
❑ Determine cue to prompt home base.
❑ Determine home base location.
❑ Identify activities that will occur during home base.

Safe Person

❑ Identify a safe person.
❑ Determine the role of the safe person, to possibly include:
  ❑ Social skills training
  ❑ Social skills interpretation
  ❑ Active listening
  ❑ Calming of the student
  ❑ Sensory support

Visual Supports

❑ Identify which supports are needed:
  ❑ Map of school outlining classes
  ❑ List of classes, room numbers, books, and other supplies

Figure 5.1. *(continued)*

❑ List of teacher expectations and routines for each class
❑ Outlines and notes from lectures
❑ Model of assignments
❑ Test reminders
❑ Schedule changes
❑ Homework instructions
❑ Cue to use home base

Travel Card
❑ Identify special educator role.
❑ Determine student role.
❑ Identify general educator participation.
❑ Define parent role.

SOCIAL SUPPORTS

Hidden Curriculum
❑ Identify hidden curriculum items.
❑ Define who will teach hidden curriculum.
❑ Determine when instruction will occur.

Circle of Friends
❑ Provide awareness training to peers.
❑ Identify peers to participate in Circle of Friends.
❑ Determine when Circle of Friends is needed to support student.

Social Skills Instruction
❑ Determine need for direct instruction:
    ❑ Identify curricula.
    ❑ Determine social skills instructor.
    ❑ Determine when social skills instruction will occur.
❑ Determine if acting lessons may support social skills instruction:
    ❑ Identify coach's need for AS awareness training.
    ❑ Provide awareness training to other student actors.
❑ Consider whether social stories are a viable means of instruction:
    ❑ Identify individual who can create social stories.
    ❑ Determine how the need for a social story will be communicated.
    ❑ Determine who will monitor social story effectiveness.

Social Skills Interpretation
❑ Determine social skills interpreter.
❑ Ensure social skills interpreter knows how to use (a) cartooning, (b) social autopsies, (c) SOCCSS, and (d) sensory awareness.
❑ Identify when student will have access to the social skills interpreter:
    ❑ Scheduled time
    ❑ As needed

Figure 5.1. *(continued)*

Student Orientation

Getting used to change and new situations is always easier and less threatening given proper advance notice and preparation. Nowhere is this truer than for adolescents with AS who are transitioning to middle or high school. As we have mentioned throughout this book, the AS student's need for routine, sameness, and predictability is severely challenged during times of change. To reduce the student's anxiety upon entering a new school at a very vulnerable age, a sound orientation program conducted well in advance of the actual transition is essential. Such orientation should include familiarization with the physical setting of the school and its grounds, introduction to all pertinent teachers and staff, and explanation of rules for behavior as well as academic performance (Adreon & Stella, 2001). As indicated in Figure 5.1, other helpful topics of student orientation include meeting with peer "buddies," sharing names and possibly photos of "safe persons," and so on.

Summary

The planning process described here may seem extensive and time-consuming. It is! For adolescents with AS, it is necessary that each of the items on the Transition Checklist be considered before the student moves into a new school environment. The complexity of Asperger Syndrome requires that parents and school professionals view all phases of the environment to ensure that modifications are in place to help the student have a successful school experience.

CHAPTER 6

A Slice of Life: Perspectives from Adolescents with Asperger Syndrome and Their Parents

Much of what we have learned about Asperger Syndrome over the years has come from individuals with this exceptionality and their parents. Therefore, we thought it would be appropriate to ask youths with AS and their parents to provide us with some insight into AS, particularly as it relates to academic and social success at the middle and high school level. The five parents (and three adolescents) who share their thoughts and experiences chose diverse but equally important issues.

In the first vignette, Jill Schmidt discusses the importance of transition planning, sensitivity, and using parents as resources. Her talented son, Jeffrey, provides insight into the type of teachers who are successful for adolescents with AS. John Oak, a 14-year-old with AS, offers some valuable information about understanding adolescents with Asperger Syndrome. Julie Tipton, whose daughter is now in college, shares experiences related to Allison's transition planning. Next, Sherry Moyer explains her decision to use homeschooling for her son Robert and describes its impact on her family. An increasingly important fear – the fear of many parents regarding their children being bullied and abused – is discussed by Rebekah Heinrichs, who poignantly describes an incident that happened to her son, Sam. Anne Briggs overviews a successful school day for her son, CJ, and then describes some traumatic incidents that served as the impetus for restructuring CJ's school experience, including providing a resource room for adolescents with AS in his school. Finally, CJ shares his thoughts and dreams in a touching poem.

To preserve the voices of the adolescents and parents who have contributed to this unique chapter, we have reproduced their thoughts and ideas in their own words with only minimal editing. We hope that what may have been sacrificed in terms of consistency in writing style and general editorial policy will have been more than compensated for in authenticity and genuineness.

Jill Osgood Schmidt – Jeffrey's Mother

As a parent who has been through every "hoop" you can imagine (right down to legal assistance for placement), there are a few things I would like to share regarding transitioning to middle school.

#1: *The rules cannot be the same for kids with AS.* One of the most important things to stress while educating students with Asperger Syndrome is that the districts need to remember that while they have teachers in place who can teach, the rules cannot be the same for our kids as for all others. By that I mean that our kids learn differently, so you have to look at the curriculum requirements and adapt them. I'm pretty tired of hearing, "This is how we do it for the other students … Don't you want to fit in?" The answer to that is NO. My son has a different way of learning and the information will always need to be presented to him in the way he learns best. I do not want my son to "be like everyone else." He is who he is and he is special to us. If information is presented to him in the way that he learns (visual supports, etc.), he will sail away with more knowledge.

Jeffrey knows there are rules and that we have to follow rules in life, but he also has learned what he needs. All he asks now is that you listen and help him. The more he knows what helps him, the better chance for success in life he'll have.

#2: *Sensitivity training is critical.* Sensitivity training is the key to the success of our kids. We have had this training in the past and the kids have been more of a support to Jeffrey than the adults because the kids will help Jeffrey, if they KNOW he has Asperger Syndrome; and they can help. We are in a situation now where we know the parents at the school Jeffrey attends will balk loudly at the "A" word

(Asperger Syndrome). This is a full-time gifted program and the children of many prestigious families attend this school (it is a public school). We have opted to be careful with the use of the term "Asperger Syndrome" here, and since the students have not experienced sensitivity training, it's been a bit difficult. Jeffrey is the first student with Asperger Syndrome in our district who is in a full-time gifted program, so we are spearheading new turf here. So far, his success has been dramatically for the better. He is in the National Honor Society and he is happy.

The advantage Jeffrey has is that he is savant in computer skills and the kids, for the most part, appear to be impressed with his expertise and tend to overlook some of the behavioral issues. Sensitivity training is something we believe truly helps in middle school. We've experienced it and it works.

#3: *Parents are a valuable resource. Please listen to them.* One of the last issues I would like to address is that of school personnel perhaps taking a moment longer to listen to parents. We KNOW they have the degrees required to teach; that is not the issue. However, we cannot expect each teacher to know everything about Asperger Syndrome – so PLEASE listen to the parents who live with the child! We don't profess to know it all, but for goodness sake, we live with these kids and through conferences, seminars, and many other ways of learning about this complex syndrome, we HAVE to try to learn what's effective for our child.

One of the comments relayed back to me by one of the resource teachers at my son's previous schools was that he is maybe only 10% autistic (insinuating that perhaps the parents were nuts!). At this, my 16-year-old son piped up, "Yeah, Mom, which toe is Jeffrey autistic in? They ought to live here!"

Listen to the parent – we're living this … we're there!

Jeffrey Schmidt – Eighth-Grade Student

My name is Jeffrey Schmidt. I am an eighth grader at a school for gifted students. I have high-functioning autism/Asperger Syndrome. I have a couple of tips on how an Asperger Syndrome child's structure needs to be when he/she gets to middle school.

First, he or she needs to have a basic schedule with rarely any changes (ex: My school has a TEAM Time/RAP schedule in which every 2nd Thursday, they add an extra period). Secondly, when one enters a middle/high school, the students in his/her environment need to have a special training so that they can understand how the Asperger student works, how she/he interprets things, sensitivity problems, social difficulties, etc. Finally, the Asperger child needs to have caring, flexible teachers that have a heart and that can understand what an Asperger child needs and how he/she thinks. For the last two years, I was at Cypress Middle School. Some teachers there listened to me, others did not (85% did not listen). Out of all two years there, 6/11 of my past teachers "removed their ear plugs" to listen to and help me. In my theory, 95% of an Asperger's teachers need to listen to him/her and advocate for the child's personal needs.

Those are some tips on how an Asperger child's middle/high school structure needs to be. All of you out there, good luck. Don't lose hope yet … for there is a light at the end of the tunnel, and a bridge to success.

John Oak – Ninth-Grade Student

My hardships going through middle school were many. One of the biggest changes was the teachers. It actually was very frightening having to go to 6 different teachers, each one expecting something different. My science teacher wanted things one way, and my language arts teacher wanted them to be another, such as how you do the heading on your work. Some teachers wanted it to be on the upper right hand and include the date, period, and teacher's name, as well as your own name, while others wanted just your name and date, but the paper had to have a title. The problem was that you could get confused and do the wrong heading and get marked down. Another change was the workload.

My years in elementary school were much easier than the ones in middle school. Not only is the work harder, but you have more of it, usually getting 1 or 2 assignments a day! You also have to worry about large projects that can sometimes be in the way of your daily work. Usually, each teacher likes to have at least 2 big projects throughout the year! This can turn out to be a problem. If they are scheduled near each other, having two projects at a time could end up being a problem.

Finally, the final big change in middle school was the students. The students in middle school seem to be more immature than the students in any other school that I have ever been to. They seem to enjoy harassing people a lot more than at other schools, by making fun of them and such. This can be extremely horrible, for you have to do your work and endure the stuff that other students do. Frankly, I wish that they would learn that that is what makes kids go berserk like at Columbine.

Luckily, I had much to help me during this time of chaos, including the support of my parents and the school employees. With their help, I was able to get through middle school, and into the high school of my choice. During 6th grade, I had problems with my temper and beat up a lot of people when they got on my nerves. With the help of the employees, I managed to stop beating up people when they gave me the ability to go out into the halls and let out some steam.

Another thing that helped me was the stress-free summers that I got to enjoy at my parents' houses. With that, I learned how to control my temper even more, and not get annoyed as much by the students. What helped me was, at my house, I don't get teased by anyone except my sister. This helped me feel much better and not get mad at anyone at school enough to beat them up. So basically, with all of the changes happening around me, I still managed to get through middle school with flying colors, with the help and efforts of many individuals.

Julie Tipton – Allison's Mother

At the beginning of each new school year, beginning when my daughter entered junior high (she is now a college junior), I would contact the school counselor or principal and arrange for a short after-school inservice meeting for all of Allison's teachers. I would also invite the bus driver and any other school personnel that Allison might spend significant time with. The meeting usually was scheduled for around the middle of the first grading period, giving the teachers a chance to get to know Allison. At the meeting, the counselor or I would present a short overview of autism and Asperger Syndrome, perhaps pass out a brochure or two, and then discuss

Allison and her unique challenges, strengths, and weaknesses as an individual with Asperger Syndrome. Teachers would then have an opportunity to ask questions or present any difficulties or concerns they might already have. Because teachers are extremely busy, invariably not all of them could attend the meeting. It would then be up to me to contact these teachers.

I found these beginning-of-the-school-year meetings very helpful in getting the school year off to a good start. I could meet the teachers, exchange phone numbers, e-mail addresses, and prep periods, and I believe they not only calmed my anxieties but those of the teachers as well. Good communication with teachers from the start is absolutely necessary – especially when one's child is totally mainstreamed as Allison was.

Sherry Moyer – Robert's Mother

In the last couple of decades, homeschooling in the United States has become an option that families are increasingly considering. Often it is for philosophical reasons such as religious ideals or dissatisfaction with the public or private facilities in their area. For our family, homeschooling was not a philosophical choice that we arrived at simply by preference. It was based on a decision made out of necessity at the end of a very bumpy road. During the early 1990s, which were the preschool years for our son, Robert showed such intellect and zest for learning that we came to count on the idea that a good school with a rigorous academic program would be perfectly suited to our needs. Unfortunately, his precocious development in the early years gave us a false sense of security. For by the time Robert was ready to begin his school career, we had started to see substantial evidence of Asperger Syndrome characteristics, even though we couldn't put a name to it.

It was not until 1994 after his first-grade year was over that we found a professional who correctly recognized Robert's condition. For at least two years before that, many of the social characteristics began to surface but they were passed over by three outside professionals and every school that he attended. It became something of a circular pattern, enrollment in May, attendance in September, problems by December and then back to enrollment in a different facility in May.

I want to be very clear that at no point in time do I mean to be critical or imply that the schools we tried did not make every effort to help us. Quite the contrary, in fact. Looking back I can honestly say that each and every person we came across during the first few years of this journey did their best to help us within the constraints of their knowledge base or particular professional focus. However, just as I would be the first person to point out that my son pushed everyone around him to the outer limits of their tolerance, they must bear some of the responsibility for not being able to accommodate him. Schools are supposed to be able to educate anyone with reasonable success, aren't they?

There should have been a place for him, except his Achilles' heel has always been his instantaneous frustration and outbursts when he perceives his world is threatened in any way. These perceptions or misperceptions, to be more precise, could be triggered in the blink of an eye and would vary from day to day causing what we now refer to in the AS community as "meltdowns." Back in the early 1990s not enough information was available about this disorder, so Robert's behavior was attributed to attention deficit disorder, obsessive compulsive disorder and oppositional defiant disorder.

Knowing what I know now, the symptoms related to those disorders could quite easily mirror AS traits, so it would not be difficult to see the behaviors as something other than Asperger Syndrome.

Second grade brought the transition to an accurate diagnosis and a public school that did everything possible to be of help. Our IEP meetings made Middle East peace summits look small by comparison. This process continued through the end of third grade with every treatment idea or educational accommodation possible being made on Robert's behalf. Still there were too many behavioral problems to count and a progressive and drastic deterioration of his test scores and skill acquisitions.

At the beginning of fourth grade Robert was transferred to a facility for students with severe emotional disturbance, and that was the end of the road for us. His emotional fragility became such that he would beg me not to make him go because this, too, was not the place for him. The chaos and volatility this created in our home life was unbearable, and at that point I decided that teaching Robert at home could not possibly be any more harmful to him than trying so hard to make him fit into the system when he just couldn't.

The choice I made at this point was to deviate from what we all know to be the "normal way" of doing things and putting my child's mental health and academic success first. The hope was also that the ripple effects of removing the stress of the school environment from Robert's life would allow for a return to some peace and balance within our family. Within two months after we took our son out of school, he had gained 30 pounds and grown three inches – not because anything else changed but there was no more monster in his mind or need for him to worry about his inability to tolerate school.

The economic reality of today's world is such that homeschooling did not come without financial ramifications. In order to make it happen, I gave up a business I had devoted three years to and we, as family, gave up our home in a fairly expensive metropolitan suburb to move to the country where things moved at a slower pace and didn't cost so much!

My son experienced frustration and outbursts or meltdowns. From my very personal experience this was one of the most difficult areas to negotiate. He expressed frustration or anger as almost a reflex reaction to situations that caused anxiety of any kind. Positive behavioral supports (PBS) was the answer to our situation.

Everything I did in homeschooling was a slightly less sophisticated version of PBS. I considered PBS to be one of my secret weapons. What better way to modify the challenging behaviors without making my child feel inept or guilty over his supposed "shortcomings"?

It took me years of spiritual growth and evolution to learn to understand that if I could just remove myself from the moment long enough to see the whole situation for what it was, I could react without ANY frustration or anger. While I still need practice and reminders to myself, I know that I have climbed this mountain because it was not too long ago, while we were doing our lessons one day, that my son began to get upset, which is usually his first, last and only response and said, "You're so calm it scares me because I never know when you are angry anymore." For me this was the defining moment of my ascendance into true adulthood. I had finally conquered what was a lifelong lesson in not getting caught up in the moment.

It occurred to me during an IEP team meeting that the general tendency for the group, myself included, was to look for what I would call an easy answer to one or more of my son's problems. I suppose it was something of an epiphany on my part but the truth is that with AS students, solving the issue at hand is more like pulling the loose end of a giant ball of string. You start with the little piece hanging out that catches your attention and pull on that until it reveals more and more of the inside of the ball, until yards later, you get to the core, or in our case the root of the problem. So my best advice was to think beyond the surface, look for the root of the problem and then do what we could to modify the child's environment to minimize the possibilities for reoccurrence.

By the time my son left traditional schooling, he had severe negative association with the concept of school. I decided that this all by itself must be conquered or school at home wouldn't be of any help either. At the time we left the school system, Robert was interested in all things rainforest so I bought a couple of tall, fake fig trees, a music CD with rainforest sounds and put colorful little plastic tree frogs on the leaves of the fig trees. For the first month we were at home together, we would turn on the rainforest music and quietly read about things of interest to him.

> **The key to successfully parenting the child with AS is flexibility and willingness to address the changing needs.**

As the month progressed, we did exercises that gave me an idea of what he could do academically but they all related to something positive for him. The idea was to change Robert's mental schema of learning to something that was not frightening or discouraging. Eventually, he became willing, if not excited, to get started each day.

After he began to view learning as a positive experience, I focused on some of the issues that caused anxiety. When working, he would commonly ask questions like, "How much time is left?" I thought he might have a problem with his ability to properly relate the passage of time. For a while, I took the time constraints out of the assignments and slowly built them back in as I saw improvements along the way. I also attempted to alleviate his anxiety by showing him how to begin a task and outline the information or steps necessary for completing large projects.

There were certain school subjects such as punctuation and spelling rules that tended to be stressors for my son. I scheduled those more frequently but for shorter time periods. I found this to be tremendously helpful because it allowed for frequent review, which will improve the long-term chances for successful learning. Following directions was also an issue, so I broke them down into smaller steps, highlighted the written ones so they stood out or repeated the verbal directions slowly and in small enough increments so Robert was able to process them.

Frequently Robert would insist that he had not sufficiently digested the material or wasn't given enough time to do so. I resorted to teaching concepts around a theme (such as the rainforest). I asked myself "What will it hurt?" After all, one of the more amazing things about my child (and others with AS) is his almost infinite ability to absorb information. I definitely didn't want to kill his love of learning; it may already have suffered some damage through his previous school years.

Like many individuals with AS, Robert has fine-motor skill deficits, which makes handwriting an unpleasant task. During his early elementary grades so much emphasis was given to learning to write properly that he was embarrassed by his poor penmanship. We were fortunate enough to have a computer in our home, so we let him type. This very visual way for the content of an assignment to be intellectually processed was an added bonus for him.

For homeschooling to work, I needed to spend some time educating myself on where to obtain home school materials and how to meet the educational requirements within my own state. There are a variety of curricula that come prepackaged so that the entire grade level is covered in different subject areas. We started out using this method because I didn't have much time to gather materials and it was very convenient. However, the drawback was that prepackaged programs can be very expensive. We now create our own curriculum to suit Robert's specific needs. I find that by using a sampling of books from different companies, I can gain a pretty good idea of what the "middle of the road" is for appropriate grade-level material. My best bet, however, turned out to be the Internet, which had no shortage of places to purchase curriculum materials.

Because I felt that my son required more services and attention than realistically possible in a system, homeschooling offered something of a haven of hope. We made some sacrifices to make homeschooling a viable option, but it has been worth the effort. At age 12, Robert no longer requires prescription medication or therapy at a time in his development when many children experience increased anxieties and crisis moments. I am not so naïve as to think this progress couldn't change at the drop of a hat but for now it is the best choice for him. Should things change in the future, we will cross that bridge when we come to it because as everyone eventually realizes, the key to successfully parenting the child with AS is flexibility and willingness to address the changing needs as they arise.

Rebekah Heinrichs – Sam's Mother

Sam is 12 years old now and in the sixth grade. He is our firstborn and full of questions and comments. He makes us laugh on a regular basis. He is diagnosed with Asperger Syndrome, but that does not define him as a human being. Sam is much more than his diagnosis, and every day we are reminded of his capacity to learn and change, which defies any label. However, having found a name for some of Sam's unique characteristics makes a huge difference in understanding and helping him face daily challenges. It enables us to be better parents and gives Sam permission to accept himself as different from, not less than, others.

Last year, a few days before school officially started, I dropped Sam off at school during the scheduled time so he could find out who was in his class and his teacher assignment for fifth grade. Before dropping him off, he told me he wasn't sure he remembered how to get home. He had walked the same two blocks back and forth to school the year before. I was shocked at his statement even though I was aware of his orientation difficulties. I reassured him of how to get home and told him he could wait for me if he wanted. I then drove the two blocks back home to pick up my daughter so she could also see her class assignment. When I arrived back at school, I didn't immediately see Sam and proceeded to help my daughter find her class list and supplies. But I soon became concerned about

Sam because I was allowing him more independence in this situation than usual. I would typically guide him through these types of activities due to his social skill deficits and poor sense of direction. In this instance, I was intentionally trying to encourage him to be more independent in an attempt to loosen my "apron strings."

When I still couldn't find Sam, I called home and my mother explained that he had just arrived and was extremely upset because he had been beaten up at school. I immediately felt guilty for leaving him alone for the few minutes it took for this happen. I kept thinking how hurt and embarrassed he must feel and what a terrible way this was to start a new school year. When I got home, Sam told me in detail what had happened, and it became obvious that he had been the victim of a cruel trick because of his lack of ability to "read" the intentions of others. Basically, another classmate his age had been unusually friendly to him and convinced him to go outside to "wrestle." The boy was with his cousin, and together they directed Sam out a side door of the school building where they would not be seen. When they got outside, Sam began going over the rules for the wrestling match but the other boys jumped him and started pushing his face down into the dirt. They wouldn't let him up and when he struggled, they choked him. He received scrapes on his forehead and bruises on his arms and his neck. They verbally taunted him and walked away laughing. Sam was scared and overwhelmed by the two of them and basically did not fight back.

When he returned inside to look for me, the mother of one of the boys involved saw Sam and asked him if he knew where her son was. Sam told her that he had just beaten him up. She then saw her son, grabbed him by the arm and left. She never asked if Sam was okay or investigated the incident. Her first instinct was to take her own child and leave. I assume she did not want him to get in trouble since the incident occurred on school property. Later when she received a phone call from the principal, she insisted that her son had simply used poor judgment in "roughhousing" on school property and that Sam was equally at fault. Because there were no other witnesses, there was no punishment even though Sam was the only one with visible injuries. Sam and the other student were both asked to write a letter of apology. I felt this would send an alarming message to Sam and refused to ask him to comply. There had been other occasions when Sam had been reprimanded for things he had been tricked or goaded into doing. This instance was of such a serious nature, however, that we felt strongly that Sam needed to know that we would advocate for him.

Sam knew this boy did not like him, I am certain, because he had just made the statement that he hoped this boy was not in his class because he had been so mean to him the previous year. I asked Sam why he trusted him when he was so uncharacteristically nice and persistent in wanting to play. Sam said he thought it was a little odd, but believed he had simply decided to be nice. I then asked Sam why he went to wrestle when we had a hard and fast rule against wrestling with friends, even in our own house. He said he just wanted to be his friend. He stated he didn't fight back because he was outnumbered and feared fighting back might anger them into hurting him more. He also knew that fighting on school property was not allowed.

Sam's inability to "read" people in social situations has always presented problems. This incident highlights his potential for victimization because of his inability to interpret the intentions of others. It is also a sad representation of Sam's desperate desire for friendship and poor boundary setting and self-esteem. This was a wakeup call to us as parents concerning the potential harm the future could present in terms of peer pressure, violence, drugs, and other issues. This is a concern that creeps into our consciousness and keeps us awake at night. Can we ever teach him all the skills he will need to make good decisions? This is a common concern for every parent. This is a constant concern in our family.

This experience left us with more questions than answers. How did this youngster know Sam could be so easily fooled? What is it about kids with Asperger Syndrome that identifies them as easy targets for teasing and worse? More importantly, what is it in others that seems to seek out the most vulnerable to attack? It is ironic that Sam is the one labeled with a social disability when he is a kind, trusting, honest person who accepts people as they are and only wants to be a friend. How sad that we must teach him how to be "careful" and not be so trusting. My hope is that other parents recognize the need to model acceptance, tolerance, and kindness in their children. If not, we will continue to see more unfortunate reminders that "the apple doesn't fall far from the tree."

Anne Briggs – CJ's Mother

CJ's typical good day starts as he gets to school 30 minutes early (I take him) to get settled in and be primed for his day. He then goes to a general education homeroom. He wants to get there early before the other kids get there – less stressful, I guess. In homeroom he is in charge of turning on the TV to watch the morning news. He is usually also the one assigned to pass things out and take things up for the teacher. He feels special.

He remains in this room for his science class. Science is his favorite subject. He participates appropriately, although sometimes too enthusiastically. He participates in lab (it's biological science) although he doesn't do much of the hands-on work when it is yucky.

Next he moves to another classroom close by for math. CJ started the year in gifted math because he has tested with a high aptitude for math. But the gifted teacher had a teaching style that was stressful for him. We also found out that the school had gifted math last year, so he had missed out on the math most of the other kids had last year, so he started the year confused. We pulled him out and put him in a small general education math class where the teacher has a more casual style. She actually gave CJ an "excellent" in conduct the last nine weeks because she likes his enthusiasm. (CJ will return to gifted classes next year in science.)

After math, CJ goes to language arts. This has been the most difficult area for him because of the writing requirements. It was the last general education class that we put CJ in. For the first half of class, he does grammar, vocabulary or spelling. The class then goes to lunch but CJ usually chooses to go back to the Asperger Syndrome resource room to eat. Sometimes kids from his classes join him. He seems to need this break in his day. After lunch he goes back to language arts; it is usually a literature or writing assignment.

Next in CJ's day, he goes to social studies where he does well. The teacher has designed the class to be predictable in that it usually follows the same format each day. I was told that CJ went up and kinda hugged the teacher and the teacher almost cried at the affection CJ showed him.

CJ's academic day is over at this point. It is now about 2:15 p.m. and CJ spends the rest of his day, until 3:30, in the Asperger

Syndrome resource room where he works on keyboarding or fine-motor and social skills. CJ has the last 1/2 hour of the day to do homework and get his reward for his behavior, which is usually time on the computer to play games.

CJ has great teachers who are enthusiastic about his progress, enjoy his personality and appreciate his intelligence – every one of them. The teachers meet weekly to go over their lesson plans, with CJ's paraprofessional and resource teachers making accommodations when needed and discussing areas where CJ may have problems and problem solving to help prevent rather than deal with problems.

It took CJ almost four months to get into all of his general education academic subjects, longer than I think it should have taken, but there were problems in the beginning. CJ lost about a month due to the stress of the gifted math class, which was unfortunately chosen to be the first class for him to start in. I have to keep on top of things every day to make sure that CJ's IEP is properly implemented. I had to push to get him out into all of the general education classes, at times going to the school myself and taking CJ to his classes. He gradually started spending less time in general education and got into the habit of not going, but I would go to school for the day and stay in class with him and he would make it through the day and start going to his classes again after that. The school has accepted me as a part of his support team. I have even taken a substitute teacher workshop and I am CJ's substitute aide when his paraprofessional has to be out. Not the best solution, but sometimes you just have to do what works. He is starting to become more independent and I can envision a day when he won't need the paraprofessional any more. I have kept the faith when those around him totally doubted his ability.

> **The school has accepted me as part of his support team.**

CJ is allowed to leave his general education classroom when he gets upset and go to the resource room to do his work. He rarely does this now, but he has been consistent in recognizing his frustration and self-calming or removing himself since the beginning of the year.

CJ has an aide with him all day. She also has educated herself extensively on Asperger Syndrome. She has a background in emotional and behavior disorders (EBD). This worried me in the beginning, but she has dealt with difficult kids and she can really appreciate how easy CJ is to handle, not the monster he was portrayed to be by earlier teachers. She can't believe they had such a bad time with CJ and agrees that EBD would be a disastrous placement for CJ.

His Asperger Syndrome resource room has a lead teacher, three paraprofessionals and six students, who spend varying amounts of time in general education. The kids in there are sweet and for the most part gentle from what I see of them.

CJ's school this year has an assistant principal of special education, who also has an EBD background. He seems to like CJ very much and they have built a friendship, with CJ going to his office to talk about football or girl problems.

An incident happened a couple of days ago that shows how great CJ is doing. CJ is very clumsy and often walks into things and people without knowing it. According to witnesses, CJ bumped into a boy in the crowded hallway between classes and the boy shoved CJ. CJ shoved him back. The other boy then threw his backpack down and punched CJ in the arm, leaving a pretty bad bruise. CJ just walked off and is quoted as saying, "I don't want to fight." Isn't that great! He didn't say anything to me until I asked about the bruise two days later. He just said it was no big deal. No one was aware of it because CJ carried on with his day as if it never happened.

If I could give advice to parents, especially moms, it would be to keep on top of what is happening at school. They need to learn their children's rights and insist on what they know is best for their child. It is hard work and can wear you down, but this is the rest of CJ's life we are shaping here and a few years of mine are well spent if that is what is required to make this work. The greatest IEP isn't worth anything if it isn't being implemented. It took some tweaking of CJ's behavior plan, but the attitude of the school is the opposite of what we experienced last year. From the principal down, everyone at the school is nice and seems to want CJ to succeed. They seem to appreciate my input and usually take my suggestions.

But at the beginning of the year all wasn't as rosy as it now appears. I do want to share with you our initial experience at the school. Before school started, I met with the general education teachers and I spent time with CJ's paraprofessional explaining CJ's disability and his strengths. Then his paraprofessional quit before school started. It was a week into school before they could hire another and I kept CJ out until they had her hired. CJ started out his first week of school pretty well, but the second week was starting to bring back bad memories. CJ was experiencing problems in math from day one. I knew he could do the work but the teacher didn't seem to agree that CJ should be in her gifted class. I was being left out and not informed, and I could see a deterioration of CJ. He complained that it was just like his previous elementary school and that the teacher was always yelling at him. Confused, I took CJ to his psychologist and he told her the same thing.

I asked for a meeting at school and received no reply. My e-mails were ignored and phone calls not returned. Then one afternoon I arrived at school to pick CJ up and the staff were outside looking for him. He had run out of his class and was hiding in the school somewhere. I looked around for a while, but decided to go back to my car out front because it was time to go home and CJ knew this. Sure enough, CJ came walking around the building and ran up to me crying. I calmed him down but the resource teacher came out and proceeded to argue with CJ while he was trying to tell me what was wrong. She would interrupt CJ each time he spoke, arguing with his version of things. After I got him calm for the third time, I told the resource teacher that I would take CJ home.

At that point I had the choice of taking CJ out to homeschool him or keep sending him back into what I knew was not an appropriate environment – possibly a damaging one. We had the perfect IEP so maybe it just couldn't be done. That was on a Friday afternoon and I thought about it all weekend. I knew I had to find out what was going on in that classroom and why things weren't working. On Monday morning, I hid a tiny tape recorder in CJ's backpack and sent him to school. I had told CJ that running away was not an option and that if he felt like he needed to run away, he was to sit on the floor and say, "I want to call my mom." They were supposed to let him call me as per his IEP. Not a great option but better than having him run away. I even told the teacher that I had told CJ to do that if he felt like running away again. We had a school meeting that afternoon so we came back early and I didn't get a chance to listen to the tape until the next day. CJ stayed in school and I received no phone calls.

When I did listen to the tape, I cried. CJ was telling the truth! He was yelled at many times. He was told that he would fail seventh grade if he didn't start doing his work. He was unable to get questions answered and was literally dragged out of the "quiet room" (which is a big closet), and all the while he was saying "I want to call my mom" – he was never allowed to call me. It was amazing to listen to the calmness in CJ's voice, as the teacher seemed to lose it over and over again. Others who heard the tape were amazed at how CJ remained in control under these circumstances. At one point he asked the teacher "are you through now?" after she fussed at him as he tried to ask a question. It was worse than I can describe here and much worse than I had imagined.

I immediately went to the school and took CJ out that day. I then called my attorney and sent him a transcript of some of the tape. As you can imagine, all heck broke loose then. We shared about 5 minutes of a three-hour tape with the school system and things started to happen. I have not regretted my actions and the consequences, which included having the assistant director of special education and a behavior specialist come to the school for the next 2-3 weeks and work with CJ and the teacher and paraprofessional to come up with a behavior plan that everyone understood – with more frequent rewards and, of course, no more yelling. (CJ's paraprofessional was out on the day of the incident so she was not involved in the abuse he took; it was the lead resource teacher who "handled" CJ that day.)

That was the turning point – I have been allowed free access to the classroom at any time since then. And CJ is allowed to call me whenever he wishes. He hasn't abused that privilege and rarely calls me anymore. I was told by the principal that the teacher was disappointed in me for taping her and felt that I had broken a trust, but I trusted them with CJ, even after their horrible treatment of him the last two years, and I felt that was the trust that was broken. I did not insist on removal of the teacher, but my contact person is now the assistant principal. The teacher has tried to make up for things but we have never spoken about the tape.

Whether it was the tape or the revelation of what was going on in that classroom, I don't know, but things did an about-face and CJ has steadily improved. We have a meeting with all of his teachers every three weeks or so and have now gotten him into all of his general education classes. He made straight A's on his last report card and is much happier. I think he has started to trust the people at his new school and some of the trauma of the last couple of years is starting to fade. He is problem solving with his paraprofessional and the assistant principal. There is still a distance between CJ and the resource teacher, mistrust on his part, I think, but it appears that she is trying very hard. He does not do well when the paraprofessional is out and the teacher accompanies him to class. That is why I am his substitute aide now.

> **We have a meeting with all of his teachers every three weeks or so.**

There is a one-day conference on Asperger Syndrome in March and all of CJ's teachers are planning to attend – general education teachers as well as special educators. They want to come!! I am planning to attend with them. Guess who is keeping CJ that day, as well as my eight-year-old? The assistant principal of special education who has befriended CJ. This is a school that cares! Please don't let me wake up!

I Am

by CJ Briggs

I am a thinker and a dreamer.
  I wonder about everything.
I hear the calmness of the waves
  from the ocean each night.
I see the beauty of the sunrise
  every morning.

I am a thinker and a dreamer.
  I pretend to be tougher than I am.
I feel what the people around me feel.
  I touch what I think should be touched.
I worry about the fate of my fellow man.
  I cry over the suffering before death.

I am a thinker and a dreamer.
  I understand who I am.
I say what is on my mind.
  I dream about a peaceful world.
I try my best to make the world a better place.
  I hope someday, someway, I will make a difference.
I am a thinker and a dreamer ....

CHAPTER 7

Michael: A Case Study

This chapter is comprised of a comprehensive case study of one young man with AS. Michael is not representative of the most "severe" case of AS, nor the mildest. However, like many youth with AS, Michael has struggled significantly when he has encountered environments that demanded skills he did not possess.

We provide you with information about Michael starting in elementary school up through his years in middle school and plans for high school. Included are substantial examples of the types of difficulties reported by Michael's parents and the professionals who worked with him. Details of the numerous meetings, memos, discussions, observations, and the development of Michael's IEP are reported to give you a realistic picture of the comprehensive and continuous support that has enabled Michael to successfully get through his middle school years.

This is a true case study. The information provided represents approximately 25% of the meetings, correspondence, phone calls, and so on, that occurred over this time period. Like many youth with Asperger Syndrome, Michael began experiencing significant difficulties during third and fourth grade.

Third Grade

Michael started third grade in a new school because his family had moved during the summer. His class consisted of 36 students and was taught by one teacher. Soon he began experiencing difficulty in a number of areas. Michael's organizational skills were poor and at times he did not complete his schoolwork. Part of the reason was that he was unable to write the homework assignments down on

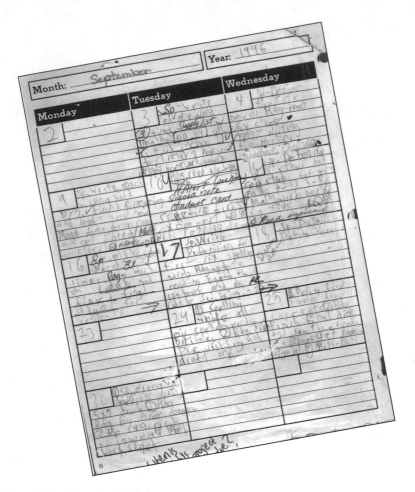

Figure 7.1. *Homework planner.*

the calendar the class used in a legible manner as there wasn't enough space for him.

To help her son, Michael's mother, Karen Nelson, designed a special homework sheet that provided more space for writing his assignments. It also included only one day on each sheet to make it less confusing. She put extra blank homework sheets in his notebook. This modification was helpful in that Michael had enough space to write down his assignments; however, it did not ensure that he wrote down the homework.

In November, Michael's mother requested her first meeting with Mrs. Kraft, Michael's third-grade teacher. Mrs. Kraft indicated that

Michael's behavior was OK in class but that it appeared that he marches "to the tune of a different drummer." She noted that Michael never seemed to pay attention when she addressed the whole class. Mrs. Nelson told Mrs. Kraft that it had always been difficult to obtain Michael's attention when he was focused on something else and suggested that the teacher might find it helpful to call him by name or tap on his desk to get his attention.

Michael's first and second quarter report cards for third grade were all "A's" and "B's." Nevertheless, his mother thought that something was wrong because "B's" were not reflective of his knowledge. Besides, he had made no friends. So after the second quarter report

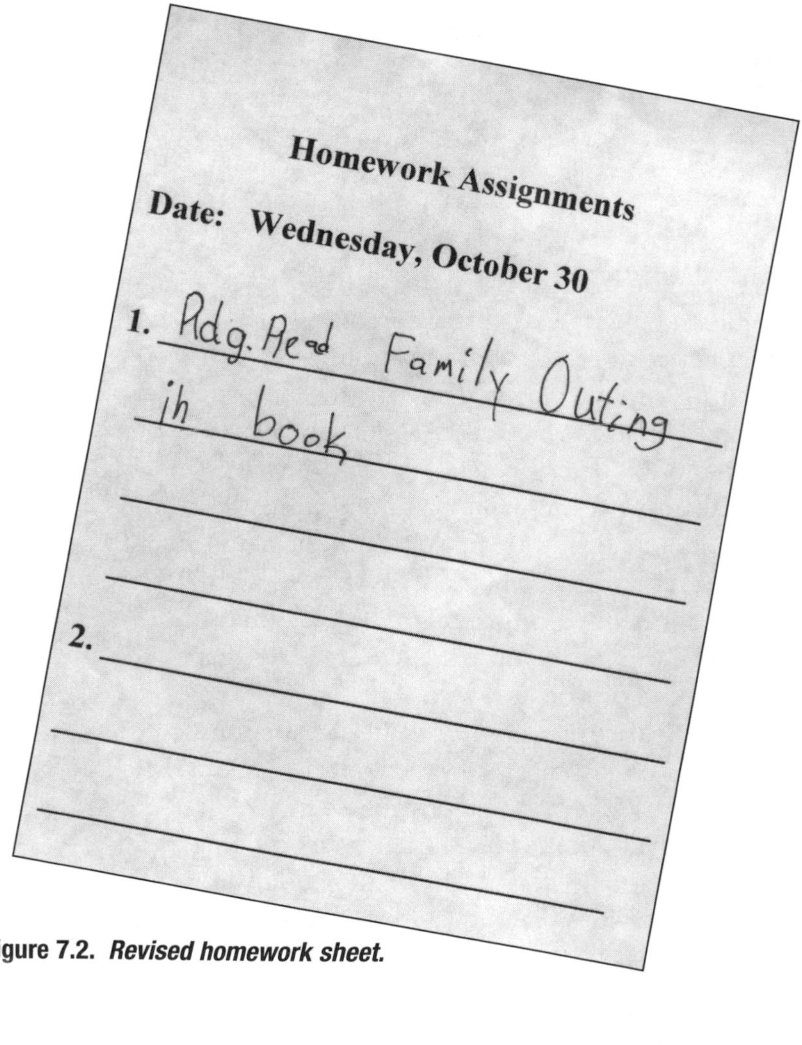

Homework Assignments

Date: Wednesday, October 30

1. Rdg. Read Family Outing in book

2.

Figure 7.2. ***Revised homework sheet.***

came home in January, she met again with the teacher. She mentioned Michael's declining interest in learning and her surprise that his grades were not better – Michael was a self-taught reader and learned to play chess before he entered kindergarten. Mrs. Kraft responded that his schoolwork did not warrant higher marks and suggested that perhaps Mrs. Nelson might like to request another teacher who had a reputation for giving out more "A's."

Unhappy with the outcome of the teacher conference, Karen Nelson requested a meeting with the school principal. Again, she expressed concern that something was wrong and pointed out that it did not make sense that Michael received a better grade in specials such as physical education and music than in academic subjects. She said that Michael appeared to have academic talents and his school performance did not reflect that.

The school principal replied that the school had high standards for grading and intimated that perhaps she was upset because Michael was not as "high-achieving" as she expected him to be. Mrs. Nelson also expressed concern that her son seemed depressed and had not developed any friendships at his new school. In particular, she was worried because Michael:

1. Seemed intensely angry over "little" things (i.e., not getting something he wanted at the store).
2. Was reluctant to talk about his feelings.
3. Didn't seem to be making any friends at his new school.
    Despite these concerns, the school took no action.

Two months later, in late March, Michael's mother received phone calls on two different occasions from the school's aftercare program about Michael's behavior. Both incidents involved Michael hitting another student who had teased him. The aftercare program was loosely structured, which might be a reason for Michael's behavior. The majority of the time the children were expected to play on the playground or blacktop with other students.

In April, Michael's mother made an appointment with a psychologist to discuss her growing concerns about Michael being depressed. She reported the following:

1. Michael had not made any friends at his new school.
2. Michael seemed less enthusiastic about learning and other favorite activities than he had been in the past.

3. Michael was saying that he disliked school and his teacher.
4. The recent aftercare incidents.
5. Michael making a few statements like "I wish I were dead" or "I'll just kill myself."

In the past Michael had always developed one or two close friendships with bright, well-behaved boys. Michael's mother thought that perhaps he was so bright that he couldn't relate to the other children.

The private psychologist, Dr. York, agreed that Michael was sad about his school situation, but was not convinced that he was depressed. He also agreed with Karen Nelson that Michael might improve if he was placed in a class where he could relate better to his peers and where the curriculum would be more engaging.

The psychologist agreed to test Michael to determine whether he would be eligible for the gifted program. He consequently administered a WISC-III (*Wechsler Intelligence Scale for Children - III*). Michael's Verbal IQ was 126, Performance IQ 134, and Full Scale IQ 135. These scores placed him in the high-average to superior range of intelligence with no significant difference between his verbal and performance abilities. The low score on the digit span subtest could be indicative of attentional difficulties, which came as no surprise.

Karen Nelson submitted the test results to the school psychologist for review and consideration of eligibility for the gifted program. School personnel met with Michael's parents and Michael was staffed to enter a gifted class for fourth grade.

Fourth Grade

Michael began the new school year in a full-time gifted fourth-grade class consisting of 35 students and two teachers. Within the first few weeks of school, Michael's parents received several phone calls concerning Michael's behavior in class. In particular, he was (a) not paying attention to instructions; (b) not keeping his papers organized; (c) not turning in homework assignments; and (d) tapping, fidgeting, and making noises.

The first week in September, Michael's mother wrote a letter to Michael's two teachers about their initial observations.

September 9, 1996

Dear Ms. McAlerster & Ms. Smith:

I spoke with Michael's psychologist about the information you shared and we compared it to last year. We agree that there is a problem. She suggested that I obtain a medical consultation as soon as possible, because we may need medical intervention to help treat his possible depression. I will begin pursuing this immediately. In the meantime, Michael is being very cooperative at home and is making a conscientious effort to complete all of his work without any fuss. He was very proud to show me the essay he wrote.

Upon your recommendation, I looked in his backpack and couldn't believe the disaster. I had only been looking in his parent folder. He has no idea of how to arrange the notebook or where to put the papers. I suggested a few weeks ago that he ask you to help him hole-punch the new notebooks, because our hole-puncher didn't work. Maybe he wouldn't ask. He has demonstrated this problem before. This past summer, he went for several days at camp without any drink at all, because he could not get himself to ask where the drinks were.

Anyhow, I will help initially to arrange his notebook. Please let me know if there are additional supplies he needs. I am trying to double-check that all the work he has done is placed in his folder. When I checked this evening, it was all falling out of the folder into the backpack. I have now attached a clip around it. One question the psychologist asked is whether you ask the whole class to turn in homework at one time. If so, it is possible that Michael does not hear the directions. If possible, please get his attention when he should turn in the work. In addition, it would be very helpful if you could take a few moments to check that he has the papers he needs to complete his work. I realize that this cannot go on indefinitely. However, he is completing 10 times more work than last year, and we have to begin building from somewhere. Also, it is possible that depression is affecting his ability to organize and pay attention.

I have given considerable thought to the noises and behaviors that Michael does from time to time, like juggling the keys. From the best that I can tell, these are not attention-getting behaviors, but behaviors that he does not seem able to control. When I ask him to stop, he apol-

ogizes and stops for a short time. Then it is as if his anxiety level goes so sky high again that he cannot help himself. As I said, I am seeking a medical consultation as soon as possible.

I know this requires great patience on the part of teachers. I believe that your class is terrific and that the academic level is right for him. Please continue to try and work with Michael while we see if we can identify some way to help him feel a bit better about himself and reduce his anxiety. This may allow him to concentrate and organize himself better and exhibit fewer anxiety-type behaviors.

Thank you so much for your assistance.

Sincerely,

Karen Nelson

Despite these efforts, Michael's academic performance and behavior at school continued to rapidly deteriorate. Foremost were his poor organizational skills. The students were supposed to write all of their assignments on a monthly calendar, but Michael did not have nearly enough room to write them down so they were legible. In addition, he seemed to have particular difficulty with writing assignments. On one assignment, he successfully completed the prewriting portion but then sat in the class for 20 minutes doing nothing. When the teacher asked him why he wasn't doing the work, he answered that he did not have a pencil. The teacher then inquired why he hadn't asked for one, to which Michael answered that he didn't think he was allowed to ask for a pencil since the teacher had told the class earlier that there was to be "no talking."

As mentioned in her September 9 letter to Michael's teachers, around this time Karen Nelson arranged for her son to see a psychiatrist. The psychiatrist met with Michael's parents, Karen and Ted Nelson, to understand how they were seeing Michael's difficulties. He interviewed them extensively about Michael's developmental history as well. The psychiatrist then saw Michael for weekly sessions for several months. Within the first few sessions, Michael was diagnosed with depression.

By the end of September, Michael's mother was becoming increasingly concerned. In a note to the psychiatrist, she wrote:

September 23, 1996

Dear Dr. Harrod,

I recently noticed that Michael cannot stand the sound of wiping a vinyl tablecloth as part of his after-dinner chores, begging me for another job. Today when I took him to religious services, he placed his hands over his ears. I told him that was rude and asked him to stop. He explained that he could not stand a high-pitched sound that was coming from the other side of the room. I gave him permission to go outside, and as we were leaving, he pointed out that the sound had something to do with the alarm system. Once I got close to the wall, I could finally hear the sound he was referring to.

Another behavior that Michael has exhibited for a long time, and that teachers (understandably) find extremely annoying, is his failure to hear anything else around him when he is engrossed in something. This has been the case for as long as I can remember. Michael's train of thought has to be completely interrupted in order for him to hear and follow any other directive. Most often, this has involved literally interrupting the stimulus (turning off the TV, removing the reading material, etc.). As a result, I guess that in class he rarely hears a group directive.

Michael continues to seem exhausted and is having trouble sleeping. Twice in the last week, he has come into my bed to sleep at around 3:00 a.m. I would appreciate any suggestions you might have.

Sincerely,

Karen Nelson

The first half of fourth grade, Michael exhibited increasingly problematic behavior in the classroom and was suspended twice, as illustrated in the following writeups from October, November and December.

Student Case Management Referral Form

Student's Name:____Michael____   Date:___October 14____

Narrative: (CLEARLY STATE WHY THE STUDENT IN BEING REFERRED)

After many conferences with student and parents, Michael did not bring in a "homework alert" slip from Friday. In class, we were practicing a writing exercise and Michael made so much noise (tapping & verbal) that two students told on him. After 40 minutes he had done nothing on the assignment.

Mary M'Alester
Signature of School Staff

Student Case Management Referral Form

Student's Name:____Michael____   Date:___October 29____

Narrative: (CLEARLY STATE WHY THE STUDENT IN BEING REFERRED)

During math (9:00 a.m.) Michael was making noises and scraping the edge of the desk with his scissors. He was told that he was destroying school property, a serious offense. A few minutes later, he started scraping his pencil with his scissors. When asked why he was destroying the pencil, his reply was, "You said not to destroy school property," in a condescending tone. He repeated this activity during reading. When this incident was discussed further with Michael, it became apparent that he thought it was alright to scrape on the pencil because it was his personal property, NOT school property.

Peggy Smith
Signature of School Staff

Student Case Management Referral Form

Student's Name:____Michael____   Date: __November 15__

Narrative: (CLEARLY STATE WHY THE STUDENT IN BEING REFERRED)

Michael was written up for "having no respect for other holidays." He drew a picture of Santa with the heading "Crismas Sucks."

Comments from Mrs. Nelson, Michael's mother: Michael was upset because of the unequal representation of Jewish decorations, songs, etc., in relation to Christian decorations. He also felt that Christian children got more presents than Jewish children. Moreover, he did not feel that he received an adequate explanation about the significance of Christmas and he wanted a Christian child to explain it, just as the teacher had requested that he explain about his Jewish holiday of Chanukah to his Christian classmates.

_____
Signature of School Staff

Figure 7.3. *Holiday drawing.*

Student Case Management Referral Form

Student's Name:___ Michael ___   Date: __ November 21 __

Narrative: (CLEARLY STATE WHY THE STUDENT IN BEING REFERRED)

Michael tends to lean back in his chair and has been told many times since September to stop. Today he was reminded three times to sit correctly, so I took his chair away. Then he started stomping on Steven's poster. I asked him to stop. When he did it again, I moved him across the room and asked him to sit at the round table. But then he started to bang on the table with his hand. I asked him to stop. He then started stomping his feet. Again, I asked him to stop, but he continued. Michael was warned that if he demonstrated another incidence of defiance, he would be suspended. Mother was called and informed.

Mary M°Alester

Signature of School Staff

Student Case Management Referral Form

Student's Name:___ Michael ___   Date: __ December 3 __

Narrative: (CLEARLY STATE WHY THE STUDENT IN BEING REFERRED)

After a lesson on being a good citizen, he started humming and chanting, "I don't understand this" over and over. This became louder and louder, so much so that Mrs. Silver, who teaches next door, came in and asked what the noise was. When Mrs. Gail, Michael's teacher, turned around, he flicked his middle finger at her.

Ellen Kraft

Signature of School Staff

Within two months, the problem behavior observed at school became significantly more evident at home as well. For example, on one occasion, Michael picked up a knife and threatened to stab himself if his mother didn't immediately go to the store and buy his favorite cereal.

Mrs. Nelson continued documenting unusual behaviors in hopes of helping the professionals understand Michael, including the following note to Michael's psychiatrist.

December 3, 1996

To: T. Harrod

From: K. Nelson

Tonight I took the children to see a musical. Prior to the beginning of the show, Michael began to repeat, "I can't see," even though we were in the second row at a tiny theatre. When the show began, he stopped, but until that time the behavior kept escalating. Shortly after the show began, he started tapping his foot on the chair of the person sitting in front of him, who asked him to stop. I had to enforce it for the rest of the show. Prior to the intermission, Michael stated that he was extremely tired and asked if he could go and sleep in the car until the show was over. His sleep patterns still seem very disturbed. He is always up early, but appears tired for most of the day. He constantly rubs his eyes and goes to bed at night on his own.

In addition, he continues to lick his joints, which are still irritated. He says it makes them feel better when he licks. It appears that it does not occur to him that this behavior is weird. Another strange new behavior has appeared. He was hot the other night in his bed, so he wrapped his body in wet towels. He liked it so much that he wanted to do it again the next night. I suggested that instead I move a fan into his room to cool him. That seemed to satisfy him.

At the recommendation of the psychiatrist, a psychological assessment was conducted to obtain additional information and to rule out any possible learning disabilities or the presence of a thought disorder. The psychological report was completed and discussed with the Nelsons on December 10, 1996. Here is the psychological report on Michael.

CENTERVILLE COUNTY PSYCHOLOGICAL SERVICES
West Area Student Services
(296) 888-2943

Psychological Assessment (11/14/96)
Name of Student: Michael Nelson

Michael has been under the care of a psychiatrist for approximately six weeks, who has diagnosed him with a major depressive disorder. The psychiatrist also reported the presence of some obsessional thoughts related to germs and contamination. Additionally, Michael is preoccupied with stories of violence and gore to an unusual degree.

Early History

Michael is the first child of two professional parents. He was the result of an uncomplicated, full-term pregnancy. He was described as a strong-willed child who exhibited irregular sleeping and eating patterns. Michael achieved developmental milestones in all areas within expected parameters. He walked at 12 months and early communication development was unremarkable. He was diagnosed with asthma at 2 years of age. By 2-1/2 he was demonstrating some advanced academic and visual-spatial skills. For example, he knew the entire alphabet and all of his numbers and was able to independently complete 60-piece interlocking puzzles. He was described as having a good attention span but exhibiting some difficulties when required to shift attention from one task to another. By age 4, he had taught himself to read, but was not yet toilet-trained. At the time Michael entered kindergarten, he often read books silently and enjoyed games such as chess and checkers.

Early School Years

Michael attended a developmental preschool and did not appear to have any significant difficulties. School reports from kindergarten through second grade were very positive.

Tests Administered

Stanford-Binet Intelligence Scale – Pattern Analysis subtest
Wechsler Individual Achievement Test

Developmental Test of Visual-Motor Integration
Connors' Continuous Performance Test
Draw a House-Tree-Person
Kinetic Family Drawing
Incomplete Sentence Blank
Thematic Apperception Test
Rorschach Inkblot Test
Children's Depression Inventory
The Piers-Harris Children's Self-Concept Scale
Personality Inventory for Children
ADHD Rating Scale - Home Version
Connors' Rating Scale - Parent Version
Clinical Interview with Michael

Behavioral Observations

Michael was evaluated during a single session. He was accompanied by his mother and easily separated from her. Initially, Michael made no eye contact with the examiner and appeared oblivious to social cues. However, he was compliant when the examiner verbally stated what she needed him to do. He was cooperative throughout the evaluation and generally put forth good effort. He became somewhat fatigued toward the end but was able to persevere when given lots of encouragement. He responded well to praise and humor. His speech was fluent and substantive. On nonverbal reasoning tasks, he demonstrated a quick, organized problem-solving style and was able to solve all the tasks. His activity level was within normal limits. During the structured testing session, his attention span was adequate but he seemed to fatigue easily as the session progressed and consequently had difficulty exerting himself on tasks. His mood seemed sad and his affect was characterized by an edgy irritability. He frequently expressed anger towards classmates as well as sadness about their rejection of him. Overall, the results of the evaluation are thought to be a valid estimate of his current level of functioning.

Test Results

The *Stanford-Binet Intelligence Scale* Pattern Analysis subtest was administered to further confirm the absence of visual-spatial difficulties. Michael responded in a quick, organized manner even to difficult items. He obtained a Standard Age Score of 67, which ranks his abilities at the 98th percentile. This score is consistent with the Performance IQ scores in the Very Superior range, which were obtained in March of 1996. There is no indication of visual-perceptual/organizational difficulties.

The *Developmental Test of Visual-Motor Integration* was administered. Michael obtained a Standard Score of 119, which is at the 90th percentile. His visual-motor integration skills are developed at the level of the average 13-year, 8-month-old youth. There are no indications of difficulties in this area.* *

*NOTE FROM THE AUTHORS: Michael has motor problems as evidenced by his writing samples. In addition, he has trouble copying from the board, writing down homework and producing written work. His performance on this test could be misleading to educators.

As a part of the psychological assessment, Michael was given the *Wechsler Individual Achievement Test*. Michael is performing at or above grade level in all academic areas. A significant strength is his reading comprehension. His mathematical computation and spelling skills are relative weaknesses.

His parents completed behavior rating scales on Michael. On the *Connors' Parent Rating Scale*, clinically significant problems appeared on all scales (Conduct Problems, Learning Problems, Psychosomatic, Anxiety, and Hyperactivity Index), except for Impulsive-Hyperactivity, which approached significant. This would indicate both internalizing and externalizing behavioral problems. His parents also reported clinically significant numbers of symptoms associated with attentional problems but not with hyperactivity. For example, Michael often fails to give close attention to details or makes careless mistakes in school work, very often does not seem to listen when spoken to directly, often does not follow through on instructions and fails to finish work, very often has difficulties organizing tasks and activities, often avoids tasks that require mental effort, very often loses things necessary for tasks or activities, and very often is forgetful in daily activities.

Computerized testing was administered to assess Michael's level of sustained attention and impulse control. Michael evidenced a high commission error rate and fast hit response rate, which is consistent with impulsivity. Additionally, he had difficulty sustaining attention across the test, suggesting problems with sustained attention as well.

Projective personality testing suggests that Michael is able to accurately perceive his environment in a conventional manner. However, he seems to experience considerable emotional turmoil, which appears to have a negative impact on his perceptual accuracy. When facing conditions of high emotional arousal, he has difficulty modulating his responses and consequently may respond in an overly emotional, disorganized manner.

Personality testing indicated a clinically significant, severe level of depression. Michael scored at the 99th percentile (T-score = 76) on the *Children's Depression Inventory* with similarly elevated scores across all subdomains. The risk of suicide needs to be carefully monitored because of the extreme amount of subjective emotional distress he is experiencing. Additionally, Michael is very pessimistic about the future and sees little hope of a positive resolution. Violence and a lack of justice for the victims characterized his stories on the *Thematic Apperception Test*.

Michael also evidenced impaired self-concept. He saw himself as inadequate across all areas. The only area approaching a normal level of self-esteem was the Intellectual and School Status subscale, which was still low (T-score=39; 12th percentile). Analysis of this scale showed that Michael views himself as smart but experiences a lot of anxiety about his ability to perform academically. Interpersonally, Michael appears to have difficulty responding to social cues and generalizing behavioral rules from one social situation to another. He expressed interest in others but sadness and anger about his rejection by his peers at school. He views his parents as providing the nurturance he needs, but appears to desire more closeness with them.

Another salient issue for Michael revolves around school. He is highly invested in his "gifted" label, which is one of his only sources of self-esteem. However, he is anxious about his ability to perform adequately academically. His stories were rife with accounts of children who wanted to do well and please the teacher but were unsuccessful. Further, the characters in his stories were often anxious about tests and homework assignments, and despite attempting to study and do the right thing, failed the tests and displeased their teacher. Michael reported a lot of anxiety about getting good grades on his report card.

Despite the reports from school of oppositional behavior, Michael appears to desire to conform to the teachers' expectations. It is possible that his high level of anxiety and his difficulty understanding social cues are the underlying factors that are creating problems in the classroom. Additionally, his severe depression is likely to make him fatigue easily and become even more irritable.

Diagnostic Impressions
Major Depressive Disorder

Attention-Deficit/Hyperactivity Disorder, Predominantly Inattentive
Type (Provisional)
Rule out Asperger Disorder*

*NOTE FROM THE AUTHORS: This language is used as an indica-
tor that an individual may have Asperger Syndrome but that it
has not yet officially been determined.

Changing Schools

Due to the significant difficulties Michael was experiencing during the first semester in fourth grade, his parents decided to change
schools in January. They felt Michael would benefit from a new setting in which the teachers and the other students did not have a pre-
conceived negative view of their son.

As a result, Michael transferred to a regular fourth-grade class
with a pull-out gifted program one day a week. School personnel
were immediately provided with information about Asperger
Syndrome. One of the things the Nelsons hoped to do was to help
school personnel understand their son, rather than attribute his difficulties to willful and manipulative behavior.

While the class work in the general education classroom was relatively easy, Michael had extensive organizational problems and difficulties writing lengthy assignments, and completing long-term
projects.

THE SCHOOL BOARD OF CENTERVILLE COUNTY, MICHIGAN
West Area Student Services
(296) 589-8300

Review Summary (February 4, 1997)
Name of Student: Michael Nelson

The school committee, which consisted of Michael's gifted
teacher, regular education teacher, school psychologist, and the
Nelsons, met to discuss Michael's adjustment to his new school
and his educational program. The classroom teacher related that
Michael sometimes forgets his homework or is not able to find it
after he completes it.

The team decided that to aid in organizational skills, a homework sheet would be instituted. They also agreed that Michael would begin working with the gifted class where he would have strategies to help him cope with his specialized problems of transitioning from one thing to another and being responsible for completing tasks. Auditory reminders of changes in his schedule would also be instituted.

The Nelsons felt positively about the review. It seemed as though school personnel were willing to communicate with them on a regular basis to stay on top of Michael's progress. The gifted teacher was to oversee the accommodations that were to be provided and to stay in touch with the regular education teacher about Michael's performance. In addition, she agreed to touch base with the Nelsons at least once a week.

Challenging behaviors continued to be observed, although not of the frequency or magnitude of the previous educational setting. To continue working with Michael, the school psychologist observed him in class, spoke with his teachers, and reported the following:

. . . *Michael rarely pays attention to what goes on in class, appears oblivious, just sits and reads a book. Will contribute factual information. Despite not appearing to pay attention, Michael did complete the work on an "A" level.*

Michael loses control very easily. For example, he shook a computer and hit it, threw chess pieces when he realized he was going to lose the game, and then cried. He often didn't seem to understand creative lessons and said things like, "I still don't understand."

He continued to tap and hum in class. On one occasion, he hit another student who had teased him about forgetting his homework and threatened to do it again. On another occasion, Michael said that he would throw a chair at people if they stared at him. He continued to exhibit poor social judgment by making comments such as "My project is the best."

After the February 4 review, a request was made by the assistant principal to the area special education office for the behavior specialist to schedule time to observe Michael. He could receive these services because he was eligible under "gifted." In addition, in March his school team developed a Behavior Support Plan for his teachers to use.

THE SCHOOL BOARD OF CENTERVILLE COUNTY, MICHIGAN

West Area Student Services
(296) 589-8300

BEHAVIOR SUPPORT PLAN   (1997)

Name:	Michael	Grade:	4
Class Size:	29	Placement:	Regular Ed.
Eligibility:	Gifted	Date:	March 3
Behaviorist:	Mary B	Ratio:	1:29
		Hours:	1 full day

Background Information

Michael is a transfer student. In his previous school, he was enrolled in a full-time gifted program. Currently, Michael is receiving services by the gifted teacher through a pull-out delivery model. Michael spends one full day a week with the gifted teacher and the rest of the time with his regular fourth-grade class. Michael feels very secure and good about himself in the gifted class. He is able to self-pace, work within a group or alone, and move about the classroom at will. In his regular education class, boundaries are set, expectations are clear, and the majority of the class assignments are done independently (seatwork). The teacher presents information clearly and uses visual examples.

Reason for Referral

The school is having some concerns about Michael in the area of social/emotional. Behaviors include excessive tapping, noise making, noncompliance, poor self-esteem, poor peer interaction, feelings that no one likes him, and at times aggression (pushing desks over). The school has requested assistance from the area

Exceptional Student Education Office for a behavioral consultation in order to better meet Michael's educational and behavioral needs.

Timelines:

February 6, 11, 26	Review of records
March 8, 28	Student observations/conferences
	Teacher conferences
	Guidance counselor conference
March 22 & 24	Parent phone conference

Interventions:	Highly structured academic & behavior-based classroom
	Rules are enforced and reinforced
	Seating changed
	Peer buddy assigned
	Increased praise statements
	Precorrection tactics attempted
	Cueing/redirecting
	Daily behavior sheet
Likes:	Computers, reading, gifted class, drawing
Target Behavior:	Refuses to follow teacher's direction, exerts little effort, makes distracting noises, interacts negatively with peers
Function:	Escape from situations Michael perceives as unpleasant
Replacement Behaviors:	Comply with teacher's direction within a set length of time, respond to social cues in an age-appropriate manner, and when bored or anxious, use specific strategies to calm himself and pace his workload
Teaching Component:	To have Michael socialize with his peers in an acceptable manner, and to develop an appropriate mode of communication when he is anxious or bored. During the school day Michael's target behaviors are most likely to occur during social situations or unpleasant activities in an effort to escape these situations. Below are some interventions for misunderstood social cues and strategies for dealing with unpleasant situations

Recommendations

1. Utilize a peer buddy for redirecting and hurdling Michael over stressful situations. Michael should also be encouraged to assist his peer buddy when deemed suitable. Empower Michael to capitalize on his strengths.
2. Within a large school setting, involve Michael in a Circle of Friends program and use social stories to foster social understanding with an emphasis on the following settings: cafeteria, free-choice time, and possible after-school activities.
3. Implement a structured social skills program that places emphasis on anger replacement and peer relations.
4. Implement a group contingency plan centered on quiet work habits. Develop a contract with Michael on a specific classroom behavior.
5. Put Michael on a visual schedule listing the activity, completion, attitude and reward. This can be done in 15- or 30-minute intervals or by activity.
6. Create an environment that reduces the number of opportunities Michael has to practice and that reinforces him for performing his challenging behaviors. Have Michael share his behavior sheet at home daily with his parents.
7. Give Michael choice time after he has completed a set number of activities or timeline. Gradually increase the amount of time or number of preset activities before choice time is given.
8. Implement self-monitoring sheet for callouts vs. hand raises. Have Michael challenge himself in a positive manner. The self-monitoring sheet will serve as a visual reminder and an incentive to participate.
9. Involve Michael in cooperative learning activities where each student in the group has a specific duty (i.e., reader, recorder, presenter, and monitor).
10. Present tasks visually rather than auditorally to better meet his learning style.
11. Implement communication-based interventions (i.e., instead of verbally acting out to escape, Michael may doodle on his paper or be taught a cue – verbal or tangible – that communicates: I do not understand, I need help, or Can I have a break?).
12. If possible, increase Michael's time in the gifted program.
13. Devise an implementation and monitoring plan with assigned roles and responsibilities.

The plan was not particularly well monitored; however, it seemed as though the teachers implemented many of the strategies.

Behavior at Home

Although things were going pretty well at school, Michael continued to exhibit low frustration tolerance at home. In March, the following incident occurred as related by Karen Nelson in a note to the psychiatrist.

March 17, 1997

To: T. Harrod

From: K. Nelson

We went through the drive-through at a fast food restaurant a couple of nights ago and realized after driving away that our order had been filled incorrectly. Specifically, Michael's cheeseburger was missing. His sister and I offered Michael our food, but he wasn't satisfied. I reminded him that he could have his soda and milkshake. Michael began escalating by repeating the phrase "I want something to eat" over and over. I told him again that he could eat from items that were in the car or that he would have to wait until we got home. Still not appeased, Michael put on the parking brake and threatened to grab the steering wheel from me. I told him that under no circumstance was he allowed to do that and, that if he did it, I would pull off the road and call the police for assistance.

Michael's sister became very frightened and began offering him anything he wanted. Michael was impatient and continued to make threatening comments, asking for a knife or some other sharp object. At the same time, he repeated that he wanted to kill his sister and cut her to pieces. I tried to calm her down, reminding her that I would always protect her. It appeared as though Michael liked to control the situation. Michael responded to one of his sister's comments by indicating that he was aware that his behavior was effective in getting him what he wanted. He also started asking me whether I would kill my son in order to save my daughter.

Determination of Eligibility for Special Education

School personnel were very concerned that Michael would require significant supports to continue to be successful, especially in moving on to middle school. Therefore, the team decided to address eligibility for exceptional student education.

Both school personnel and the Nelsons were concerned that without documentation and a "thinking set" focusing on developmental disability, Michael would be viewed primarily as emotionally handicapped or severely emotionally disturbed. The school personnel suggested that the Nelsons allow the school to gather additional information and review Michael's records to determine whether he met criteria for exceptional student education and, if so, under what category(ies).

In early May, the Nelsons signed consent forms for school personnel to assess Michael using various autism and behavioral rating scales, speech and language standardized and informal assessments. They also consented to a review of outside evaluations previously completed on Michael. In addition, the Nelsons gave the school psychologist a letter dated April 29, 1997 from Michael's psychiatrist, along with a copy of Dr. York's psychological assessment (date of evaluation: 11/14/96).

In a letter dated May 8, 1997, the psychiatrist wrote the following:

. . . For over a year Michael has been suffering from dysthymia and, more recently, a superimposed major depression. He also shows significant attentional problems and the diagnosis of attention deficit hyperactivity disorder – primarily inattentive type – is under consideration. During the course of the evaluation and now early treatment, it has become evident that Michael demonstrates impairment in social interaction and restricted patterns of behavior and interests. For these reasons, he carries the provisional diagnosis of Asperger Syndrome. The combined impairments caused by his depression, probable pervasive developmental disorder and inattention, have resulted in his current marked difficulty in performing up to his capacities in the classroom and explain his behavioral problems.

In addition to the report from the psychiatrist, significant problems were recorded by the school psychologist on the *Childhood Autism Rating Scales* in the areas of Relating to People, Emotional Responses, Adaptation to Change and Nonverbal Communication. On the *Autism Behavior Checklist,* difficulties were noted in the areas of Relating to Others, Social, and Self-Help.

Eligibility for speech and language was also assessed. As a result, Michael was administered the *Test of Problem-Solving – Revised.* He received a standard score of 108. Pragmatic observation checklists completed by his parents, gifted teacher and fourth-grade classroom teacher, indicated a severe social and pragmatic language deficit.

Since eligibility is based on the checklist, not the standard score, the team met to address eligibility for exceptional student education in June 1997, at the end of fourth grade. The team decided to place Michael under "autism" in order to develop an Individualized Education Plan (IEP) and lay the groundwork for transition planning.

Strategies that were developed the previous year were continued, including verbal reinforcers, adult reinforcement of appropriate understanding of situations and responses, an area to "chill out" (home base) if needed, and social skills training.

Interim Review: June of Fourth-Grade Year

The committee met to discuss Michael's progress and plan for the following year. They agreed that the teacher should be hand-picked, somebody whose style is calm and organized, yet flexible.

Training of the teacher would occur prior to Michael's arrival. This training would be provided by outside consultants specializing in autism and AS. Incorporated into the teacher's training were the following:

- Providing the student with additional space around his area (bus, work, assemblies, etc.). Michael was usually placed at the back of the class so his movements/noises would be less distracting to other students. In addition, for assemblies the class sat at the side of the bleachers so Michael could be on the end and thus have additional space. When lining up, each student had a number and lined up by number.
- Providing a daily assignment sheet

- Teaching keyboarding skills in special education class
- Trying to avoid placing him in situations that would frustrate him
- Avoiding power struggles
- Building in peer awareness by having the teacher explain to the class that Michael had a disorder he was born with. The teacher will point out that he will be treated differently because he learns in a different way
- Capitalizing on Michael's "better" social skills with younger students by having him be the gifted teacher's assistant with another age group one day a week. (This also provided a "break" for the general education teacher.)
- Establishing a pass system. When Michael would begin to lose control, he would be prompted to go to an established place
- Giving Michael choices. Writing is usually an area of weakness for students with Asperger Syndrome. This was true for Michael as well. However, the gifted class wrote the school newspaper and Michael was given considerable latitude in writing on areas of particular interest to him
- Using visuals to assist Michael in understanding assignments, projects, learning activity packets

A new set of goals was established to be distributed to all staff who comes into contact with him.

A range of hours will be instituted in both the gifted and the special education setting. Michael will be going to the special education setting and/or gifted program for independent study, individualized computer work and special group activities, which may include social skills, student tutoring and time in a different setting.

THE SCHOOL BOARD OF CENTERVILLE COUNTY, MICHIGAN
West Area Student Services
(296) 589-8300

Exceptional Student Education

Individualized Education Plan:
Gifted Eligibility

Name of Student: Michael Nelson

Area of Need
Responsibility, social, emotional needs.

Present Level of Performance
Michael is a bright boy who is having difficulties in social situations.

Annual Goal
To accept responsibilities for tasks, learn to ask for help when needed, and learn to be part of a group.

Short-Term Instructional Objectives
1. Michael will try to learn to be a participant in group activities.
2. Michael will learn to ask for help when needed, in the classroom, in specials, and in the cafeteria.
3. Michael will learn to give a "warning" when he becomes agitated. This warning will be "telling the teacher" rather than breaking out into physical violence.
4. Michael will learn keyboarding skills so that written tasks may be easier for him.

Comments
Michael's progress report in the third and fourth quarters of his fourth-grade year indicated that he "needs improvement" in the following areas:
- Listens and follows directions
- Completes class work in assigned time
- Stays on task

- Works well with others
- Obeys class rules
- Respects rights and property of others

He was marked satisfactory in the following areas:
- Completes homework within assigned time
- Thinks and works independently
- Respects authority
- Accepts responsibility

His grades in all subjects were "B's" and he was marked satisfactory in art, music, and physical education.

In Michael's gifted class, he completed most of his work independently.

Summer

Over the summer break, Michael attended a day camp. The campers picked special areas of interests and participated three days a week "on-campus" and two days a week "off-campus." Michael chose the following areas of focus: (a) computer, (b) bowling, (c) golf, and (d) science. Before the start of camp the Nelsons met with the directors and familiarized them with AS. The agency sponsoring the camp had a policy of working with students with special needs, and decided to put an additional staff member in Michael's group for "off-campus" days. The summer camp experience was successful for Michael.

Fifth Grade

Considerable planning took place before Michael entered fifth grade as outlined in the previous pages. Despite implementation of the recommended modifications, Michael soon began to experience difficulties in the classroom.

In October Michael's teachers expressed concerns about controlling his behaviors when he gets upset with peers. When he feels other children are laughing at or teasing him, Michael becomes violent, pushing desks and hitting others. The teachers recommended that Michael learn "coping" skills and perhaps strategies that would include a "warning" before he gets out of control. To help Michael work on these areas, the following IEP was developed.

THE SCHOOL BOARD OF CENTERVILLE COUNTY, MICHIGAN

West Area Student Services
(296) 589-8300

Exceptional Student Education

> **Individualized Education Plan:**
> **Gifted and Autism Eligibility**
> **October, 1997**

Name of Student: Michael Nelson

Area of Need
  Responsibility, social-emotional needs.

Annual Goal
  Michael will continue learning strategies to work responsibly both independently and with a group.

Short-Term Goals
  Michael will work with other children in a small-group setting learning strategies to work as part of that group. Michael will learn to establish his own goals and chart his progress as he works toward goal completion.
  • Michael will use and organize alternate materials for in-depth projects of special interest to him.
  • Michael will learn keyboarding skills, practicing on a regular basis, so that written tasks may be completed with less frustration.

Area of Need: Social/Emotional/Language

Annual Goal
  Michael will continue working on strategies to lessen his frustration level.

<u>Short-Term Objective</u>

Michael will participate in a social skills group to work on strategies to improve his social skills (discontinued in group format).

- Michael will learn to ask for help when needed so that his internal frustration doesn't mount.
- Michael will learn to use school resources when he becomes agitated – for example, a warning like telling the teacher, taking a break, or going to a special place.
- When anxious or confused, Michael will seek clarification in order to better understand the situation.

On his second quarter report card, Michael received all "A's." His teacher had been successfully implementing many of the suggested strategies and his response had been positive. Thus, in some ways, Michael's report card was a reflection of the school's ability to individualize his educational program to his needs. For example, his teacher frequently allowed Michael to complete projects on his own rather than with the group. On the report card, one area was still marked "needs improvement." Not surprisingly, that was the area of "works well with others."

January 1998 Incident

The committee met to discuss Michael's progress and the incidents that had resulted in Michael losing his temper and reacting violently in his regular classroom.

In one instance, an administrator came to the classroom to deliver donuts to students who had actively participated in singing the "12 Days of Christmas" at the school holiday party in January. The students had not been informed beforehand of any consequence for singing/not singing. Since Michael had not joined in the song, he did not receive a donut. He consequently threw a chair across the room.

The committee was concerned for now and for future behavioral episodes and wanted to help Michael learn to use immediate measures before he loses his temper. A new behavior plan with intervening strategies was developed to include the following:

1. The school social worker will meet weekly with Michael to discuss confidentially what's on his mind and to engage in positive practice of using a card or pass to move away from a frustrating situation.
2. The substitute behavior strategies will be reviewed and practiced by Michael and his teachers and also at home.
3. When Michael uses this strategy he should be rewarded, possibly with candy.
4. If Michael becomes violent, he will be referred to an administrator who will call his parents.

It was decided that, if necessary, the administrators may remove Michael from school for the rest of the day or use external expulsion when deemed necessary and after the parent has been contacted. Previously utilized strategies and supports for Michael will continue. A discussion of middle school options was initiated. Testing for the gifted mathematics program was suggested, including a practice session to prepare Michael.

May 1998 Incident

Michael was suspended for two days, allegedly for physically hurting another student by picking him up and throwing him to the floor. This incident occurred when the other student walked by Michael and accidentally hit him in the head with his elbow. Michael thought the student had hit him on purpose.

Transition Planning for Middle School

Transition planning for middle school was fairly extensive, starting in the spring of Michael's fifth-grade year. The parents, program specialist, gifted teacher, and behavior specialist visited several schools to see which program would benefit Michael the most. These included the neighborhood middle school, a Montessori magnet school, and a science magnet school.

The neighborhood middle school was rejected due to the reputation of the administration as being extremely inflexible with problem behaviors and because of the typical middle school curriculum used there – students working at desks doing traditional paperwork rather than active hands-on learning with labs and computers and access to other higher-technology materials.

The Montessori magnet program had a receptive special education staff. In fact, they were interested in getting a student with Michael's academic strengths because the majority of their students were low achieving. But one of the drawbacks of the program was that there were no academic requirements for enrollment. As a result, the program attracted a number of students who scored poorly on standardized tests and students who needed remedial work in math and reading. Historically, Michael has been most successful socially with bright high-achieving peers. A large portion of the population included students with "black street language," which would be difficult for Michael to understand. In addition, it was felt that those students would have difficulty understanding Michael's pedantic speech. The overall impression was that Michael would not fit well with the student population at the school.

The science magnet school was also considered. The school was equipped with significant technology equipment and labs, and had an extended schedule of field trips to provide students with exposure to a wide range of experiences.

Several of the staff from Michael's grade school felt that he might do reasonably well in a program with particularly bright, somewhat nerdy, students. In addition, Michael had seen a videotape on magnet programs and had stated that he was interested in attending the science magnet program.

To be considered for the magnet program, Michael had to meet their admissions criteria of scoring in the top 75th percentile on the *Stanford Achievement Tests*. This was no problem, as Michael's SAT scores all fell in the high-90 percentile rank.

After Michael was admitted, Mr. and Mrs. Nelson and school personnel met with the coordinator of the program, as well as the exceptional student education specialist, to candidly discuss the kinds of supports Michael might need. Several weeks later a transition planning meeting was held to plan the transition to the new school. Included in the meeting were representatives from Michael's elementary school (gifted teacher, behavior specialist, and area program specialist), a representative from the district transportation department, a district program specialist, the behavior specialist for the new school, the magnet coordinator, exceptional student education specialist, inclusion support personnel from the magnet program, and Michael's parents. The magnet coordinator wrote a report summarizing some of the decisions and main points from the meeting, which were distributed to the support team.

General impressions

Tests well; excellent reader; likes to assist slower students; emotionally immature; only works well with an encouraging peer; works well independently; if calm, will raise hand – if not calm, watch him closely; needs help interacting with others; wants to be liked; rigid; doesn't always ask questions; look for rocking – don't ignore; needs a routine; needs to be counseled regarding handling academic disappointments.

Situations where Michael may have problems
- *Crowding*
- *Being touched or bumped into*
- *Teasing*
- *Feeling discriminated against*
- *Change in routine*
- *Pressure or anxious situation*

Signs that Michael may be experiencing problems
- *Making faces*
- *Making noises*
- *Rocking*

Things to do if a problem presents itself
- *Make him recognize you*
- *Divert his attention*
- *Ask him to leave the room and do an errand, or go to the library*
- *Work with him on the problem as it is happening*
- *Prepare him if something out of the ordinary is going to happen*
- *The best thing to do is to raise his self-esteem. Punishment may have the reverse of the desired effect*

Based on these observations, the team made the following decisions:

Transportation: Michael will sit in the front seat behind the driver. The bus driver will report any instances of teasing/bullying or any other concerns to school personnel.

Elective: Michael will serve as the media aide for the first semester.

Behavior Plan: The behavior will address the following:
- Development of pass system
- Assistance with homework planner
- Alternative arrangements and/or supports many be needed during unstructured times/transition periods. Upon arrival, Michael will report to the media center or the special education office.

A series of meetings were scheduled to take place over the summer, involving Mrs. Nelson, the special education specialist, the inclusion support teacher, a behavior specialist from the area, and an outside consultant with expertise in Asperger Syndrome. In addition to developing a Behavior Plan, the group designed a pass system, planned Michael's orientation prior to the first day of school, and arranged staff training for the week prior to school.

Meeting to Develop Behavior Plan

Behavior specialists asked Michael's parents to complete a functional analysis interview form. Responses indicated that Michael had problems when he was frustrated, interrupted or surprised. He also had difficulty in social situations – especially when he thought something was unfair or when the rules did not make sense to him. His parents viewed Michael as very sensitive to teasing and bullying. Mr. and Mrs. Nelson indicated that Michael's favorite activities included video games, movies, reading, drawing and computer. They reported that Michael disliked physical activity, writing on topics that were not of interest to him, and working with students he did not like.

The Nelsons described Michael's major behavior problems as "reacting impulsively in situations where he misunderstands the situation or feels boxed in." In these instances, he may become violent or uncooperative. These behaviors happened most frequently under circumstances when Michael was "hit in any way," if something was taken from him, if he was teased, if he was subjected to unexpected changes, when his sensory needs were not met or when there was a lack of clarity and expectations and he did not have sufficient knowledge of what to do.

The Nelsons noted that they could usually tell when their son was going to lose control by looking at his facial expression, which they characterized during this time as angry or tense. In some instances, Michael made comments about something bothering him, but the amount of distress was not adequately conveyed by his tone of voice, body language and facial expressions. Therefore, they have learned to pay careful attention to his words. The Nelsons indicated that Michael was often unable to let them know what he needed or wanted. They usually had to listen carefully to his comments or seek more information when they saw signs of stress.

As a result of this meeting, a rudimentary pass procedure was devised. When it appeared that Michael was losing control, he could ask to use his pass or the teacher could suggest that he use his pass to leave the room, or go to home base.

Michael's Orientation Strategies

In addition to the standard tour of the incoming school with other magnet students, two weeks prior to the first day of school, the following took place:

- Michael participated in an individual tour of the school with a representative from Exceptional Student Education
- Tour was videotaped
- Michael received his schedule
- Michael walked through the actual schedule
- Seating was assigned and Michael tried out assigned seating in each class
- Bus procedure was explained
- Cafeteria procedure was explained
- Michael received photographs of each teacher, labeled with the teacher's name and subject area
- Michael completed maps of the school, marking routes from various classrooms to the special education office, as well as to

bathrooms from various locations around the school
- Procedure for leaving class and going to the bathroom was addressed
- Pass procedure was explained

Staff Training Prior to First Day of School

The magnet team received a one and one-half hour orientation on Asperger Syndrome. All school personnel (including office staff, security, cafeteria workers, etc.) were informed about Michael and the pass procedure.

Sixth Grade

Supports for First Weeks of School

Supports were implemented throughout the day to facilitate Michael's adjustment to his new school. These included:
- Parents dropped Michael off and brought him inside for the first few days.
- Support personnel escorted him to each class to monitor transitions.
- Support personnel monitored lunch period.
- School personnel monitored class dismissal and waiting period until Michael boarded the bus.

Initial Problem Behaviors Prior to "Crisis" Analysis and Plan

During the first weeks of school, Michael's parents spoke on numerous occasions with the support personnel to check on how their son was doing. The teachers were not reporting any problems to support personnel, so they assumed everything was progressing well.

But shortly before Thanksgiving, Mr. and Mrs. Nelson received an interim report stating that Michael was significantly behind in some classes. This was a major sign that they were nearing a crisis. When they contacted school personnel, the staff thought they were overreacting. However, several behavioral incidents occurred within the next weeks that made it clear to everyone that Michael was having increasing difficulty in several areas. Some of the behavioral incidents were as follows.

INCIDENT REPORT

December 7

Michael came into class and slammed his fist on the desk. Threw three textbooks and tore up my teaching materials. Parent contacted: Parent agreed to replace books.

Kevin Baker

Signature, Social Studies Teacher

INCIDENT REPORT

December 14

Michael refused to move his seat after continued problems with peer sitting across from him. I gave him a choice to move or said I would speak with his dad. When I went to call his dad, Michael appeared to move but then he exploded by kicking away his chair and picking up another chair and throwing it across the room, hitting an aquarium. I then suggested that he use his pass; he found it and left the room.

Joe Wilson

Signature, Science Teacher

By the end of December, the school had assigned an aide to Michael for the entire day. However, the situation was not improving. In a meeting with support personnel, teachers, and Michael's parents, it became clear that the staff were not recognizing early signs of stress. For example, in one instance Michael exhibited tapping behavior and excessive noise making over three class periods, yet no one intervened or reported the behavior to support personnel.

Problems with Pass System

One of the problems that had occurred shortly before winter involved an incident in which the teacher felt Michael had been given the option to use his pass but had not done so. This incident occurred in his math class. Michael mentioned to the teacher that it was "too noisy." His math teacher reminded him that he could use his pass if he wanted to. But according to the teacher, the next thing that happened was that Michael threw his math book on the floor.

Upon further examination, the team noted that Michael did not demonstrate the ability to recognize his emotional status and initiate removing himself from the classroom prior to a "meltdown." Therefore, a plan was developed (as part of the positive behavioral support plan) to teach him to use his pass. Michael was told that using his pass when prompted was a desired behavior. Further, when he removed himself, he would be able to help himself to a piece or two of his favorite candy, which was kept in the special education office. He would not be marked down on any grades for having to leave class and he would be able to make up all missed work.

A simple system of prompting was established, including the use of clear language such as, "This is your first prompt to use your pass." "This is your second prompt to use your pass." Use of the pass was not to be presented as a "choice" for Michael because it appeared as though he became "stuck" when his anxiety level was too high and then was unable to make a decision. Part of the plan was that if Michael did not respond to the second prompt, security would be called and he would be removed from the classroom. If security were called to remove him, he would not receive candy once he arrived in the special education office as he would be considered to have violated "the rule."

The behavior specialist practiced by having teachers prompt Michael to leave the classroom in situations with low stress. Successfully responding to the teacher's prompt resulted in praise and getting his favorite candy. Gradually, the pass was used in "stressful" situations.

Once the team was trained in recognizing Michael's early signs of stress and used a clear prompting system, school personnel never had to physically intervene to remove Michael from a class. Throughout, the Nelsons communicated with staff as they noted problems in maintaining Michael's supports.

Many of the incidents that occurred were not formally written up, making it difficult to determine the contributing antecedents/setting events. School personnel felt strongly that Michael must receive some consequences for inappropriate behaviors; therefore, he was assigned three Saturday suspensions for various incidents. On these occasions, Michael was to report for three hours under the supervision of an administrator. He was assigned to perform various tasks throughout the school with other students, who were also suspended.

The outside behavioral consultant recognized that without careful planning, the suspensions could greatly increase the problems Michael was experiencing. Therefore, the Nelsons set up a meeting with school personnel to discuss the accommodations that might be needed. First of all, the administrator needed to be someone who was familiar with Michael and understood his communication and socialization challenges. The problems in pairing Michael with "typical," non-magnet students who were on suspension were discussed as well as the degree of supervision that would be necessary for Michael's safety. It was decided that Michael would be given tasks to complete alone with close supervision from a familiar staff member. With these conditions agreed upon, Michael completed the Saturday suspensions without any behavioral incidents.

Functional Analysis

Over the winter break, an extensive functional analysis interview was initiated and completed by an outside behavioral consultant with expertise in autism and Asperger Syndrome in an attempt to identify some of the variables that were contributing to Michael's downward spiral.

In planning for the interview, the interviewer was careful to consider times/conditions when Michael was most willing to answer questions; for example, after meals or snacks, after engaging in a preferred activity, and so on. In advance, he was given monetary reinforcement for willingly participating in the interview. Finally, Michael was reminded that the information gathered in the interview would help teachers and staff understand some of the things he found challenging.

The following are the actual interview responses, as well as a summary of information obtained from the functional analysis interview. The results of the interview provide numerous clues to what to observe when school resumes after winter break, additional information to obtain, and supports to consider implementing.

Functional Analysis Interview
Name of Student: Michael Nelson

Period I: Computer Class
- Doesn't understand teacher's feedback
- Has to move away from seat to copy information
- Can't see overheads on board from seat

Period II: Math
- Difficulty copying from board
- Can't read items written in red or yellow
- Hesitant to speak up because people may make fun of him
- Won't write out the process in math homework assignments; needs step-by-step breakdown to do so
- Sad about not working with his friend, Justin
- Unclear how homework is given

Period III: Science
- Doesn't understand teacher's feedback
- Problems with two peers calling him names. One has whiny irritating voice, the other kicks him under the table. One of these peers sits next to him in class
- Behind on science project
- Was so overwhelmed he wouldn't give parents copy of assignment
- Worried about failing the class and being kicked out of the magnet program
- Got an "F" on the interim test

Period IV: Language Arts
- Can't read teacher
- Has difficulty with the manner in which spelling tests are given
- Difficulty understanding assignments
- Unfair assignments (choice, amount of information available)
- Writing assignments are difficult

- Highly dislikes writing assignments
- Teacher keeps moving his seat
- Student currently working alone, but given same amount of work as group of four. Feels he is being punished for working alone
- Homework given verbally

Period V: World History
- Homework given verbally
- Sometimes doesn't hear assignment and gets a zero

Hypotheses about the Relationship Between the Environment and Michael's Behavior
- Michael's behavior is more likely to occur when he is showing signs of frustration.
- Michael's behavior is less likely to occur when he is in a highly structured situation, is current on all academic demands, and has positive relationships with those around him.
- Michael's behavior is maintained/reinforced by the ability to reduce/remove stress/internal reduction of anxiety.
- Michael's behavior is reinforced/maintained by escaping or avoiding highly stressful situations.

The Nelsons and their private behavioral consultant were concerned that school personnel would react too slowly in pulling together resources to help reverse the downward spiral Michael was beginning to demonstrate, so they sent a strong and very specific memo to the school with copies to administrators at the district level.

MEMO

December 28, 1998

To: *Mrs. Fowles (special education specialist); Mrs. Gallagher (behavior specialist); Mr. Campbell (inclusion support facilitator); Mrs. Frew (autism support specialist)*

cc: *Mr. Shade (district special education program planner); Mrs. Thompson (district autism supervisor)*

From: *Karen Nelson and Ms. Fasser, private behavioral consultant*

When an individual with Asperger disorder is in crisis, the priority is stabilization. To stabilize the school environment, we must increase supports immediately and reduce stressors. To stop the escalating crisis, we must reduce anxiety. The goal is to help Michael successfully survive every day.

We also need to lower expectations. This is not a time when Michael is capable of learning new tasks. Eliminate discussions of feelings, self-assessment and other abstract topics such as asking him, "What do you think you can do to handle this situation more appropriately?" These topics only serve to increase anxiety. Additionally, postpone self-assessment of classes and teaching him to use his pass.

Remove Stressors
- *Keep Michael away from problem peers (in helpful manner, not punitive)*
- *Limit amount of required work*
- *Reduce difficulty of work*
- *Change as little as possible (schedule, seating, assignments, people)*
- *Reduce writing assignments*
- *Simplify all tasks involving organizing, planning, and sequencing by breaking them down into small tasks and providing direct assistance*
- *Do not emphasize the relationship between performance on assignments and impact on grade*

Add Supports
- *Maintain consistency. If you have to change something, prepare Michael ahead of time*
- *If a variable changes, further reduce expectations/demands following the change*
- *Stabilize seating*
- *Allow access to peers Michael likes with support of school personnel (remember that his judgment is impaired and his tolerance is low)*
- *Provide written homework assignments*
- *Capitalize on Michael's strengths and interests by adapting assignments and giving as much choice as possible*
- *Increase reassurance, praise, and clarification of teacher feedback*

- *Consider arranging for Michael to speak with adults he likes at school about his favorite topics. This may enable him to feel connected to school personnel and increase a general feeling of safety and well-being*
- *Reassure Michael that the school staff will provide him help in successfully completing the language arts project and the science project. Discuss the projects with him in a positive manner*

In response to this letter, Mrs. Gallagher, the behavior specialist, suggested that Michael be the focus student for a positive behavioral support team. She drafted the following plan, which was reviewed at a team meeting on January 4, 1999. Mrs. Gallagher also arranged for the inclusion support teacher and behavior specialist to observe Michael on January 3, the day he returned to school following winter break.

SCIENCE CLASS OBSERVATION
(Inclusion Specialist) 1/3/99

Comments: Michael did very well and worked the entire class. He did need to be verbally reminded a couple of times, but when he was reminded, he complied and did his work.

Michael seems to be paired very well in class. I was excited to see him writing down due dates in his planner and was also glad to see him raising his hand to inform his teacher that he was finished with his abstract. The teacher did a great job of checking the dates Michael wrote down, reminding him to start, and checking on him the one time he showed signs of stress.

Recommendations: When giving verbal directions, make sure Michael is listening. Provide the class with a schedule for the day and remind them (Michael) when it is time to move on to the next thing. For example, Michael was reading from his journal and started to write when told to do so. A schedule would help him remember to do both, as well as a class reminder to start writing at a specific time.

The following draft was developed by the behavior specialist at Michael's school to assist school personnel in developing and implementing a behavior intervention plan for Michael.

Functional Behavioral Assessment/Positive Behavioral Support Plan (Draft)

Name of Student: Michael Nelson

Support Team Members

Exceptional student education specialist
Behavior specialist
Secondary autism support teacher for the area
Outside consultant with expertise in Asperger Syndrome
Michael's parents
Inclusion support teacher
Coordinator of the magnet programs

Information and Data Collection

Information and data were collected by a behavior specialist, resource teacher, autism specialist, special education specialist, and outside consultant with expertise in Asperger Syndrome.

Data collection included review of records and evaluation information, unstructured direct observation, structured direct observation, student interview, parent interview, teacher interviews, parent recommendations and teacher reports.

Goals of Interventions

The following goals will help enhance Michael's performance by allowing him to access education at the level of intelligence he possesses:

1. Michael will be able to demonstrate appropriate behavior within the classroom setting when feeling stressed.
2. Michael will improve his completion of academic class work, homework, and projects.
3. Michael will be able to read the social cues of his assigned teachers.
4. Michael will be able to use strategies that will help him calm down when feeling frustrated.

Environmental Adjustments

1. Present all homework in written form to Michael. It must be written in black (not red) marker. The homework can be placed on an overhead, the board or a homework sheet or planner (in the same way and same place every day).

2. Present daily classroom schedule, as detailed as possible, in written form to Michael at the start of each class. Note and explain in detail any changes to the standard classroom procedures, seat changes, or presentation style. Please include any assemblies, fire drills, guest speakers, or other nontypical activities.

3. Seat Michael in the back of the room with other peers. He should be interviewed by the teachers to pick out appropriate peers whom he would like to sit by. The same applies to group work. Place him with the same group of peers consistently. Any changes, including team changes, should be discussed in detail with Michael beforehand to help the transition.

4. Give lots of specific, consistent feedback on how he is doing. Michael does not pick up on social cues like other students. This is one of the most important suggestions. Give lots of specific, labeled praise.

5. Break ALL assignments into small parts and provide a finished example, if at all possible.

6. Extend the amount of time to complete an assignment or allow Michael to take the work home to complete (please write this on the daily report so parents are aware of the situation).

7. Tape a list of rules dealing with stress and behavioral guidelines for the classroom into the back of Michael's notebook for him to review before each class. Prompt Michael to look at the rules in the book at the start of the class.

8. Ensure that all directions are very specific and conduct a comprehension check after all major items. Do not ask yes/no questions. Make Michael demonstrate or explain back to you what you want him to do.

Behavior Management Procedure

All teachers need to be aware of and actively look for signs of frustration from Michael. These are as follows:

- Head down
- Lack of eye contact
- Rubbing face, head, and hands
- Facial grimaces
- Rocking in chair

Once <u>any</u> of these observable signs is seen, the teacher is to DISCREETLY get close to Michael and try to get him to:

- Tell what he should be doing
- Demonstrate what he should be doing

If these options don't work, ask questions to help clarify what he should be doing. In addition, try to:

- Reduce the work to bring down stress for a short time
- Notice and point out things Michael is doing correctly
- Praise him

If all attempts fail, call the office for Mrs. Campbell (inclusion support specialist), Mrs. Fowler (special education specialist), Mrs. Jones (magnet coordinator), or Mrs. Gallagher (behavior specialist). Please remember that by the time observable signs are seen, Michael's frustration is already extremely high.

Skills to Be Taught

- Social skills stories will be used to help teach Michael how to reduce stress and observe the social cues of specific teachers. Mrs. Campbell (inclusion support teacher) will teach the story once a week.
- Positive practice for using a pass at times of high frustration will be started. Michael will use the pass once a day during calm times to feel more comfortable using it under stress. A reward will be given after each use of the pass in an appropriate manner, under stress or otherwise.

Home-School Communication

- Michael will use his daily planner in each class. Teachers and parents will sign the book. Teachers will prompt Michael to bring the book up at the end of the class. Teachers will write about any missed work, late assignments and behavior every day. Teachers will give a printout of weekly grades at the end of each week.
- A copy of all long-term assignments, test dates and any major projects will be placed in Mrs. Campbell's (inclusion support teacher) box.

A few days after the draft was developed, school personnel met with each teacher to go over the positive behavioral support plan. A couple of weeks later, a meeting was convened to update Michael's IEP, which was due for an annual review.

The School Board of Centerville County, Michigan
West Area Student Services
(296) 589-8300

> **Annual IEP Review**
> **January 19, 1999**

Annual Goal
- Michael will demonstrate appropriate behavior within the classroom setting when feeling stressed or frustrated.

Short-Term Goals
- When frustrated, Michael will utilize his emergency pass.
- Michael will use his planner for clarification of daily and long-term assignments.
- When presented with a socially inappropriate situation, Michael will seek adult assistance.
- With the use of social stories, Michael will be able to utilize a teacher's social cues in the classroom.
- Michael will improve his ability to complete class work home-work and projects within the required time frame.
- Within a cooperative learning group, Michael will work as an equal partner.
- Within a cooperative learning group, Michael will demonstrate socially appropriate behaviors (i.e., ask peers for role clarification, ask for clarification from peers when he doesn't understand their comments).
- Within a cooperative learning group, Michael will demonstrate leadership abilities.
- When presented with a class assignment project, Michael will verbally state/paraphrase the requirements of the assignment.

Annual Goal
- Michael will improve his ability to complete class work, home-work and projects within the required time frame.

Short-Term Goals
- When uncertain of a task or assignment, Michael will ask for clarification from his teachers.
- When given a project or long-term assignment, Michael will break it into three steps with teacher assistance.

Desired School/Post-School Outcome
- Complete middle school/high school programs leading to four-year degree.

Based on the educational impact of the disability, the priority educational need(s) for the duration of the IEP include:

Priority/Educational Needs
- Michael will improve his ability to complete class work, homework and projects within the required time frame.
- Michael will demonstrate appropriate behavior within the classroom when stressed or frustrated.
- Michael will effectively communicate his needs to students, teachers and parents in school and at home.

Accommodations (the following are needed for all classes)
- Provide preferential seating
- Break lessons into smaller segments
- Provide extra time for processing/responding
- Provide extra time for assignments
- Allow use of computer, word processor for responding (as needed)
- Use daily reporting and collaboration with the parent
- Teach organizational strategies
- Provide regular feedback and progress check

Transportation Need
- Closest, safest pickup on regular bus
- Seating in front of bus
- Give own seat on bus

Academic Adjustments
- Homework presented in visual form (i.e., overhead, board, or homework sheet) same way, same place, every day. Planner is acceptable.
- Daily classroom schedule as detailed as possible presented at the start of each class in visually clear form. Changes in classroom procedures, seat changes, or presentation style should be specifically noted and explained in detail. Please include assemblies, fire drills, guest speakers, and other special activities. At the end of class period, check daily planner.
- Seating assignment will be in close proximity to teacher or in area not distracting to classmates.

- Long-term assignments will be placed in support facilitator's mailbox.
- Teachers need to give lots of specific feedback to Michael about how he is doing.
- Teacher should interview Michael to help pick peers with whom he would like to sit. The same should be done for any group work. If group work is to be done, try to place Michael in a group of peers he likes. Place him with the same group of peers consistently. Any changes, including team changes, should be discussed in detail beforehand with Michael to help with the transition.
- All directions need to be specific with comprehension checks after all major items. Do not ask yes/no questions. Make Michael demonstrate or explain what you want him to do.

Mr. and Mrs. Nelson continued to have problems around the issue of homework. In late February, they wrote the following memo to school personnel on the matter..

MEMO

To: *Special Education Specialist, Inclusion Support Facilitator*
From: *Karen and Ted Nelson*
RE: *Michael*
Cc: *Autism Specialist, Behavior Specialist*
Date: *2/22/99*

A number of problems regarding homework need to be addressed promptly.
1. *It is an ongoing problem that Mrs. Martin, Michael's language arts teacher, wants him to write down the complete week's homework assignments. He becomes overwhelmed by seeing the assignments for the entire week. Why don't we just provide him with a written copy of all homework? Does she put it on an overhead? If so, she can photocopy it. We need to adapt where it is easy, so we can save the energy of both school personnel and Michael. We discussed having teachers write homework assignments for him if he was having a problem writing it down himself. However, this is not in the IEP or in the Notes section. We think we should reconvene the IEP team to add this adaptation.*

2. *We are not aware of and/or understand all the homework Michael is being assigned. Possibly, Michael is feeling so overwhelmed that he is afraid to show us the list of assignments. How about faxing the homework to us on a daily basis?*

3. *We were not informed about the long-term project in history class. Michael should receive an extension on any long-term project when the information has not been conveyed immediately to Mrs. Campbell (inclusion support facilitator) and us.*

4. *We must establish a system for evaluating all assignments given to Michael and look at alternatives. There continue to be problems with the types of assignments he is given. It is unclear whether the teachers are informing Mrs. Campbell as agreed. It may be necessary to have Mrs. Campbell review all assignments.*

   Please note that our knowledge as parents is limited to information we obtain from Michael. If the information we have received from Michael is correct, there are inherent problems in these assignments for a student with Asperger Syndrome. Therefore, additional assistance is required or alternative assignments need to be considered. Once again, Michael has expressed concern about these assignments and how to do them. The time delay in addressing homework problems adds to Michael's anxiety.

5. *Specifically, assignments of concern include:*
   * *a language arts essay on fears*
   * *a social studies project involving a drawing and a poem, "Put feelings into it like Renaissance writers did"*

   Michael has expressed that he does not know how to do these assignments. He doesn't know when the project is due, how to approach it, etc. We spoke to him about asking Mrs. Campbell for help, but as we know, he may not do so.

6. *It has also come to our attention that Michael needs assistance in learning how to write paragraphs when researching a topic. He understands it for creative writing but seems confused when writing his science report. Mrs. Martin, his language arts teacher, explained to him that you begin a new paragraph when you have a new idea. For him the entire report is on one topic. He doesn't seem to understand the breakdown of subtopics.*

As a result of this memo and the Nelsons' request, the IEP team was reconvened. It was agreed that homework assignments would be faxed to parents on a daily basis and that approximately once a week, the inclusion support teacher or behavior specialist would arrange to observe Michael in various settings throughout the school day. This would be a part of the ongoing monitoring, since it was often difficult for Michael's regular education teachers to recognize a problem until it became major.

During one of these "spot checks," the behavior specialist observed the following.

LUNCHROOM INCIDENT
& INTERVENTION

3/1/99
Lunchroom Observation: 12:30-12:40 p.m.

Michael sat at a table in the cafeteria next to a broken chair. Another student insisted on putting his things on that chair. Michael repeatedly asked the student not to put anything there. When the student put something on the chair, Michael pushed him.

- Student next to him put feet on broken chair between them.
- Michael told student to take foot down.
- Student laughed; then took foot down. Talking to other peers and laughing, student put foot back.
- Michael looked at his food, then at the student's foot. Then he pushed student's foot off the broken seat. This happened three times.
- Other students laughed (I had to intervene).
- I talked to Michael about the situation and how he can only control himself: Use pass, take tray to my office to eat, switch seats, go tell staff.
- I walked Michael to class after the lunchroom problem and observation. He stood up when everyone else was in seat. Sat alone when given choice to come to my office or pick a seat. Michael chose to go to the behavior specialist's office for about 10 minutes and then returned to class.

The following week, the area autism specialist wrote an outline of a "social story" for the inclusion support teacher to work on with Michael. The outline included suggestions of sections where she might want to obtain Michael's perspective and write it into the story.

After the inclusion teacher wrote a social story with Michael, the autism support teacher taught her how to use the concept of social stories to assist Michael in learning appropriate lunchroom behavior.

A copy of the social story follows.

Social Story - Lunch

I have a new lunch period. I have to go to a new lunch period because my schedule has changed. My new schedule allows me to be an assistant/aide in the media center. I really like working in the media center.

There are certain things about this new lunch period that are different:

1. I need to use my pass so I can be one of the first persons in line with my food. This way I will have plenty of time to eat my lunch and not have to worry about being late to class.

2. After I get my lunch, I need to go to my seat. The table by the administrators usually has room. I also know the administrators and can talk to them when they are not busy.

Sometimes a person or something going on in the lunchroom may be bothering me. If this happens, there is a set way for me to handle the problem. These are ways that I need to handle problems:

If another student is doing something that bothers me, the first thing I should do is use my words and ask him to please stop. Sometimes the student will listen to my words. It is nice when other students listen to me and help me, but they do not have to always listen to me. Sometimes students do not want to listen to my words. I need to remember that I cannot make them listen to me. If another student will not listen to my words, there are some things I can do but there are also things I cannot do.

I Can:
-Leave the situation
   (go to another seat,
   go to the special education
   office, go to the
   media center)
-Use my words

I Cannot:
-Touch another student
   (push, hit)
-Touch another student's
   belongings
-Force others to honor my
   requests

Despite all precautions and accommodations, incidents continued to occur. On the last day of school, one of the other students sprayed blue hair color on Michael's hair and Michael repeatedly punched him. Both students were suspended for the day.

Seventh Grade

The biggest challenge throughout seventh grade was trying to get school personnel to keep Michael's parents informed about his homework assignments. As agreed earlier, they were supposed to be faxed home on a daily basis, but often the fax machine couldn't handle the load or the support teacher didn't get the assignments from the teacher. Since it was often unclear to Michael and his parents what the homework entailed, there was almost daily communication back and forth to clarify requirements.

Another ongoing challenge was the reporting system for when Michael got behind in work. To help resolve this situation, Michael's math teacher and the support facilitator began corresponding through e-mail with Michael's parents, which was extremely helpful. The following are examples of their correspondence.

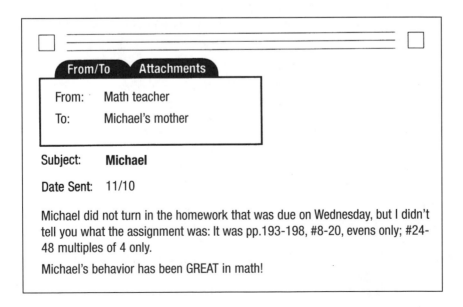

From/To   Attachments

From: Math teacher
To: Michael's mother

Subject: **Michael**

Date Sent: 11/10

Michael did not turn in the homework that was due on Wednesday, but I didn't tell you what the assignment was: It was pp.193-198, #8-20, evens only; #24-48 multiples of 4 only.

Michael's behavior has been GREAT in math!

From/To   Attachments

From: Michael's mother

To: Inclusion support teacher

Subject: **Clarification of science work**

Date Sent: 11/13

Michael spent a few hours at the library with the sitter and they could not find any information on the satellite he had picked. He still cannot find a picture of it either. He spent over three hours on-line but couldn't find any. Apparently, he searched under satellites, rather than space (and didn't ask for clarification). We're going to have to brainstorm on academic supports, because what we've got in place is not cutting it. I think we need a methodical plan for organization alone – a system and supports for the beginning and end of every class, every day, until it becomes routine.

End-of-Year Reevaluation

In May, at the end of seventh grade, Michael was reevaluated.

THE SCHOOL BOARD OF CENTERVILLE COUNTY, MICHIGAN

West Area Student Services
(296) 589-8300

Exceptional Student Education

IEP Reevaluation

Student: Michael Nelson
Age: 13-6
School: Boone Magnet
Grade: 7
Report Date: 5/16/2000

Reason for Referral

Reevaluation is required every three years. Michael is a special education student with gifted, autistic (Asperger Syndrome), and speech/language eligibilities. The last report was dated 5/5/97. An update in the areas of academic achievement and processing is requested.

Background Information

Please see prior reports for pertinent background information. Michael's parents completed the parent information form for reevaluation. This document indicates that Michael gets along well with all family members. Discipline, when seen as fair and appropriate by Michael and the consequences are anticipated, is accepted by him. In his leisure time, Michael enjoys watching videos, the computer, music, collections, and science. Difficulties for Michael are reported to be developing close friendships, unusual fears and worrying a lot. His parents feel that school staff is supportive and have provided accommodations for Michael, but that Michael "needs to function more independently." They would like to see "more direct instruction in specific areas and better evaluation of necessary schoolwork."

Assessment Procedures

Woodcock-Johnson Psychoeducational Battery-Revised (WJ-R)
Wide Range Assessment of Memory and Learning (WRAML)

Behavioral Observations and Impressions

Michael separated easily from his classroom on both testing sessions. He was interested in telling the examiner that his house had been robbed. During the second session, Michael spent considerable time talking about a new game system he had just received, Dream Cast, and again, about the robbery at his house. When asked about his summer plans, Michael indicated that he is negotiating with his parents to get several games instead of going to camp, as this would be much more economical in the long run. During the math portions, Michael asked if he could use a calculator, indicating that otherwise it could take him a long time. He noticed and commented on the distractors in the applied math problems. When presented with sentences to be written, Michael frequently asked for clarification or for additional information.

Tests Results and Interpretations

Woodcock-Johnson Psychoeducational Battery-Revised (WJ-R)

Tests of Achievement

(Administered on 5/2/2000)

Cluster Scores	Grade Equivalent	CA &ile	Standard Score
Broad Reading	11.9	90	120
Broad Mathematics	11.0	84	115
Broad Written Language	11.1	83	114

Subtest	Grade Equivalent
Letter-Word Identification	10.7
Passage Comprehension	13.0
Calculation	8.3
Applied Problems	13.8
Dictation	8.0
Writing Samples	16.9

Michael's academic skills are more than three years above his current grade placement. His overall reading skills are on a late eleventh-grade level, with higher reading comprehension. He is able to recognize the following isolated typewritten words: significance, bouquet, apparatus, trivialities. Michael's math skills are on a beginning eleventh-grade level, with higher skills when applied in practical settings. Michael is able to add and subtract fractions with like denominators and reduce fractions to their simplest terms. He is able to calculate square feet, interest, and percentages. In written language, Michael is able to write the abbreviation for et cetera and spell the words arrogance, bizarre and millenniums. His written sentences are quite detailed and include proper punctuation.

Wide Range Assessment of Memory and Learning (WRAML):

Subtest	Scaled Score
Picture Memory	8
Design Memory	9
Verbal Learning	9
Story Memory	11
Memory Screening Index	95

Michael performed better on tasks with auditory cues in context than on a short-term memory task involving visual details. His overall memory skills are within the average range of functioning.

Despite doing well overall, Michael continued to have occasional behavioral outbursts. Mr. and Mrs. Nelson felt Michael's school year had been fairly successful. They admitted that they were looking forward to the summer as a time for Michael and themselves to "recuperate."

Eighth Grade

Michael continued to perform well in school. School personnel provided clear ongoing communication between teachers and parents. Specifically, homework assignments were e-mailed to parents on a regular basis and support staff checked with Michael's teachers weekly to find out if there were any outstanding assignments. By now most of the support staff knew Michael well. He, in turn, trusted them and felt that they liked and supported him. The following e-mails are samples of the communication that occurred regularly between school personnel and Michael's parents.

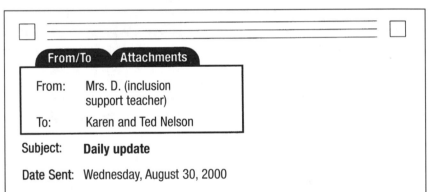

From/To   **Attachments**

From: Mrs. D. (inclusion support teacher)

To: Karen and Ted Nelson

Subject: **Daily update**

Date Sent: Wednesday, August 30, 2000

Ms. B. (Michael's language arts teacher) has requested sending Michael's updates directly to you via e-mail and sending me a copy. I've given her your e-mail address. Mr. N. (history teacher) is reviewing the Code of Conduct book this week for a test on Friday.

Ms. P. is not giving homework this week.

By the end of the day, Ms. H. will let me know how Michael did today. If it's anything you need to know for tonight, I'll send another e-mail.

You may wish to add this address to your address book, as I am mailing it directly from the school board e-mail system rather than my home AOL account.

From/To   Attachments

| From: | Mrs. B.
(language arts teacher) |
| To: | Michael's parents |

Subject: **Michael's assignments**

Date Sent: Thursday, August 31, 2000

Good morning!

I'm very excited this year. I am in the building instead of out in the portables so I get to take advantage of all the wonderful technology our school has to offer. This means that I can e-mail you Michael's assignments and also keep you informed if he should be missing any work or if I notice anything that I feel bears watching. Best of all, I can notify you of anything immediately. So far this week, we have been doing primarily housekeeping tasks such as supplies, forms, etc. Today I will be giving them their first assignment.

The students will create an acrostic poem using their name. Using the letters in their name as the first word of each line (visuals in class to copy if necessary), their poem is supposed to reveal something of themselves such as hobbies, character traits, etc. They will also decorate each first letter to further reveal something about themselves. Then they will present their poem to the class. I will speak with Michael about his feelings regarding presenting. My guess is he'll ok, it but I won't push it. It's an introductory activity so the students and I can get to know one another as well as an intro to the rubrics I often use for scoring.

Expect to see the rubric today and a literature book – which Michael may leave at home – today or tomorrow.

Thank you for your time.

From/To   Attachments

From: Mrs. D.
         (inclusion support teacher)

To: Michael's parents

Subject: **Daily update**

Date Sent: Thursday, August 31, 2000

As I mentioned to you Monday morning, I gave Michael two folders to assist him with organization. The red one is for homework that needs to be completed ("Stop and do the work."). The green folder is for finished work ("Go hand it in.").

In math, Michael has a short assignment: page 17, problems 22-25.

In science, Michael has to do the section assessment, page 19, problems 1-5. Due tomorrow (Friday). Mrs. H. reports that Michael has performed well this week. He has completed two research and oral presentations in class this week.

Have a nice evening!

From/To   Attachments

From: Mrs. B. (language arts teacher)
To: Michael's parents
CC: Inclusion support teacher

Subject: **Michael**

Date Sent: Tuesday, September 5

Today, 9/5, we presented our acrostic poems and Michael wasn't quite prepared. Fortunately, we had more students than time would allow to present, so Michael will get the extra day he needs to complete this assignment.

I gave him the choice of presenting his poem or not.

If we set up a system at school to make sure Michael is writing down his assignments and due dates in his home planner, and you look at this at home, I think we can help him come closer to meeting assignment deadlines.

Tomorrow, 9/6, we will continue to present our poems and then the students will do their first free writing in their composition books.   Thank you.

From/To	Attachments

From: Mrs. B. (language arts teacher)
To: Michael's parents
CC: Mrs. D. (inclusion support teacher)

Subject: **Assignments 9/7**

Date Sent: Thursday, September 7

Michael turned in his acrostic poem and chose not to present. He did a nice job from a cursory glance. I will inform you of the grade when I have it.

Michael was assigned to read in his lit. book. He must answer Q's 1, 2, & 5 on page 12 and complete "Writer's Notebook" in his composition book.

The textbook should have been brought home Wed 9/6 and left home until year's end.

The improved system of communication regarding homework assignments, along with the positive social-emotional supports provided by school personnel, helped Michael continue to improve his school performance. The Nelsons knew what homework was assigned and were able to reinforce Michael for responsibly writing down his assignments, bringing home the necessary materials, and completing work in a timely manner. His second quarter grades for eighth grade were as follows:

Broad Communication: (Media Aide)	A
Advanced Language Arts	B
Algebra	C
Science (Research)	B
Advanced Science (Applied)	C
Advanced U.S. History	A

Knowing the importance of planning ahead when it comes to their son's education, the Nelsons have been actively gathering information about possible high school placements. Michael would automatically be accepted into the science/preengineering high school magnet program. However, he has expressed an interest in computer technology. His school district offers three special programs in computer technology. One is in a school with an especially rough student population, so school personnel has strongly encouraged the family to explore all options.

To date, Michael has attended an Open House at two of the three potential placements. In the meantime, the Nelsons have arranged daytime visits to all three schools, as well as meetings with coordinators of the magnet programs and the special education specialists at the schools. Michael is most interested in one of the schools, because it would enable him to take Japanese as an elective. The schools allow "shadowing," that is, the potential student can spend a day at the school paired with a student currently enrolled in the program. Michael did not want to shadow at any of these schools. He was afraid he might get lost. Planning his orientation to his new school prior to the first day will be essential to reduce his anxiety. Orientation will include familiarizing him with the staff and the physical environment.

The Nelsons know that they will need to continue to strongly advocate for Michael. It will be up to them to insist that Michael's team receive training to understand him better. In addition, they need to stay in close contact with school personnel to ensure that the accommodations are taking place and that Michael does not fall behind on his schoolwork. The Nelsons also know that they must monitor Michael's emotional status and remain on the lookout for any problems with teasing and bullying by peers. With all of these pieces in place, they are hopeful that Michael will survive the next few years and successfully complete high school.

References

Adreon, D. (2000, Winter). Organizational supports. *FASTimes, Florida Asperger Syndrome Times,* 1.

Adreon, D., & Stella, J. (2001). Transition to middle and high school: Increasing the success of students with Asperger Syndrome. *Intervention in School and Clinic, 36,* 266-271.

Alspaugh, J. W. (1998). Achievement loss associated with the transition to middle and high school. *The Journal of Educational Research, 92,* 20-25.

American Psychiatric Association. (2000). *Diagnostic and statistical manual of mental disorders* (4th ed. text rev.). Washington, DC: Author.

Anderman, E. M., & Midgley, C. (1997). Changes in achievement goal orientations, perceived academic competence and grades across the transition to middle-level schools. *Contemporary Educational Psychology, 22,* 269-298.

Arowosafe, D. S., & Irvin, J. L. (1992, November). Transition to middle level school: What kids say. *Middle School Journal, 23,* 15-19.

Arwood, E. L., & Brown, M. M. (1999). *A guide to cartooning and flowcharting: See the ideas.* Portland, OR: Apricot.

Autism Asperger Syndrome Resource Center. (1997). *Assessing the setting demands in the classroom.* Kansas City, KS: Author.

Ayres, A. J. (1979). *Sensory integration and the child.* Los Angeles: Western Psychological Services.

Barnhill, E. (2000). *Attributional style and depression in adolescents with Asperger Syndrome.* Unpublished doctoral dissertation, University of Kansas.

Barnhill, G., Hagiwara, T., Myles, B. S., & Simpson, R. L. (2000). Asperger Syndrome: A study of the academic profiles of 27 children and adolescents. *Focus on Autism and Other Developmental Disabilities, 15*(3), 146-153.

Barnhill, G. P., & Myles, B. S. (in press). Attributional style and depression in adolescents with Asperger Syndrome. *Journal of Positive Behavioral Supports.*

Bieber, J. (Producer). (1994). *Learning disabilities and social skills Richard Lavoie: Last one picked . . . first one picked on.* Washington, DC: Public Broadcasting Service.

Black, S. (1999). Major school transitions require more than a one-shot orientation. *American School Board Journal, 186,* 53-55.

Bromley, K., Irwin-DeVitis, L., & Modio, M. (1995). *Graphic organizers: Visual strategies for active learning.* New York: Scholastic.

Cumine, V., Leach, J., & Stevenson, G. (1998). *Asperger Syndrome: A practical guide for teachers.* London: David Fulton.

Dunn, W. (1999). *The Sensory Profile: A contextual measure of children's responses to sensory experiences in daily life.* San Antonio, TX: The Psychological Corporation.

Dunn, L. M., & Dunn, L. M. (1981). *Peabody Picture Vocabulary Test – Revised.* Circle Pines, MN: American Guidance Service.

Dunn, W., Myles, B. S., & Orr, S. (in press). Sensory processing issues in Asperger Syndrome: A preliminary investigation. *The American Journal of Occupational Therapy.*

Durand, V. M., & Crimmins, D. (1992). *Motivation Assessment Scale.* Topeka, KS: Monaco & Associates.

Gerler, E. R., Drew, N. S., & Mohr, P. (1990). Succeeding in middle school: A multimodal approach. *Elementary School Guidance & Counseling, 24,* 263-271.

Goldstein A. P. (1997). *Skillstreaming the adolescent (revised).* Champaign, IL: Research Press.

Grandin, T. (1999, April). *Understanding people with autism: Developing a career makes life satisfying.* Paper presented at the MAAP Services, Incorporated, and Indiana Resource Center for Autism Conference, Indianapolis.

Gray, C. (1994). *Comic strip conversations: Colorful, illustrated interactions with students with autism and related disorders.* Jenison, MI: Jenison Public Schools.

Gray, C. (1995). *Social stories unlimited: Social stories and comic strip conversations.* Jenison, MI: Jenison Public Schools.

Gray, C., & Gerand, J. D. (1993). Social stories: Improving responses of students with autism with accurate social information. *Focus on Autistic Behavior, 8,* 1-10.

Green, R. W. (1998). *The explosive child: A new approach to understanding and parenting easily frustrated "chronically inflexible" children.* New York: HarperCollins.

Harris, L. G., & Shelton, I. S. (1996). *Desk reference of assessment instruments in speech and language.* San Antonio, TX: Communication Skill Builders.

Hartos, J. L., & Power, T. G. (1997). Mothers' awareness of their early adolescents' stressors: Relation between awareness and adolescent adjustment. *Journal of Early Adolescence, 17,* 371-389.

Henry Occupational Therapy Services, Inc. (1998). *Tool chest: For teachers, parents, and students.* Youngstown, AZ: Author.

Hook, D. L. (2000, September 10). Mom in the middle. *Kansas City Star,* H-1, H-8.

Howlin, P. (1998). *Children with autism and Asperger Syndrome.* New York: John Wiley and Sons.

Jones, V. F., & Jones, L. S. (1995). *Comprehensive classroom management: Creating positive learning environments for all students* (4th ed.). Boston: Allyn and Bacon.

Kadesjo, B., Gillberg, C., & Hagberg, B. (1999). Brief report: Autism and Asperger Syndrome in seven-year-old children: A total population study. *Journal of Autism and Development Disorders, 29,* 327-332.

Kasselman, C. J., & Myles, B. S. (1988). Getting the most from a lecture: Strategies for teachers and students. *LD Forum, 13*(4), 15.

Kennedy, C. H., & Fisher, D. (2001). *Inclusive middle schools.* Baltimore, MD: Paul H. Brookes.

Kern, L., Dunlap G., Clarke, S., & Childs, K. (1994). Student-assisted functional assessment interview. *Diagnostique, 19*(2-3), 29-39.

Kerr, M. M., & Nelson, C. M. (1993). *Strategies for managing behavior problems in the classroom.* Columbus, OH: Merrill/Macmillan.

Kientz, M., & Miller, H. (1999). Classroom evaluation of the child with autism. *AOTA School System Special Interest Section Newsletter, 6*(1), 1-4.

Lewis, T. J., Scott, T. M., & Sugai, G. (1994). The problem behavior questionnaire: A teacher-based instrument to develop functional hypotheses of problem behavior in general education classrooms. *Diagnostique, 19,* 103-115.

Little, L. (2000, Fall). Peer victimization of children with AS and NLD. *The Source: A Publication of the Asperger Syndrome Coalition of the United States, Inc.,* 1, 6.

McIntosh, D. N., Miller, L. J., Schyu, V., & Dunn W. (1999). *Short Sensory Profile.* San Antonio, TX: The Psychological Corporation.

Michael Thompson Productions. (2000). *Social language groups.* Naperville, IL: Author.

Mizelle, N. B. (1990). *Helping middle school students make the transition into high school.* Champaign, IL: ERIC Clearinghouse on Elementary and Early Childhood Education. (ERIC Document Reproduction Service No. ED 432 411)

Mullins, E. R., & Irvin, J. L. (2000). Transition into middle school. *Middle School Journal, 31,* 57-60.

Myles, B. S., Bock, S. J., & Simpson, R. L. (2000). *Asperger Syndrome Diagnostic Scale.* Austin, TX: Pro-Ed.

Myles, B. S., Constant, J. A., Simpson, R. L., & Carlson, J. K. (1989). Educational assessment of students with higher-functioning autistic disorder. *Focus on Autistic Behavior, 4*(1), 1-15.

Myles, B. S., Cook, K. T., Miller, N. E., Rinner, L., & Robbins, L. A. (2000). *Asperger Syndrome and sensory issues: Practical solutions for making sense of the world.* Shawnee Mission, KS: AAPC.

Myles, B. S., & Simpson, R. L. (1998). *Asperger Syndrome: A guide for educators and parents.* Austin, TX: Pro-Ed.

Myles, B. S., & Simpson, R. L. (2001). Understanding the hidden curriculum: An essential social skill for children and youth with Asperger Syndrome. *Intervention in School and Clinic, 36,* 279-286.

Myles, B. S., & Southwick, J. (1999). *Asperger Syndrome and difficult moments: Practical solutions for tantrums, rage, and meltdowns.* Shawnee Mission, KS: AAPC.

Nowicki, S. (1997). *Instructional manual for the receptive tests of the Diagnostic Analysis of Nonverbal Accuracy 2 (DANVA2).* Atlanta, GA: Author.

Occupational Therapy Associates Watertown. (1997). *Adolescent/adult checklist of occupational therapy.* Watertown, MA: Authors.

Odegaard, S. L., & Heath, J. A. (1992). Assisting the elementary school student in the transition to a middle level school. *Middle School Journal, 24,* 21-25.

O'Neill, R. E., Horner, R. H., Albin, R. W., Sprague, J. R., Storey, K., & Newton, J. S. (1997). *Functional assessment and program development for problem behavior: A practical handbook.* Pacific Grove, CA: Brooks/Cole.

Phelan, P., Yu, H. C., & Davidson, A. L. (1994). Navigating the psychosocial pressures and adolescence: The voices and experiences of high school youth. *American Educational Research Journal, 31,* 415-447.

Reis, S. M., Burns, D. K., & Renzulli, J. S. (1992). *Curriculum compacting: A process for modifying curriculum for high ability students.* Storrs, CT: The National Research Center on the Gifted and Talented.

Reisman, J., & Hanschu, B. (1992). *Sensory Integration – Revised for individuals with developmental disabilities: User's guide.* Hugo, MN: PDP Press.

Richardson, R. C. (1996). *Connecting with others: Lessons for teaching social and emotional competence.* Champaign, IL: Research Press.

Rinner, L. (2000). *Asperger Syndrome and autism: Comparing sensory processing in daily life.* Unpublished master's thesis, University of Kansas.

Schumacher, D. (1998). *The transition to middle school.* Champaign, IL: ERIC Clearinghouse on Elementary and Early Childhood Education. (ERIC Document Reproduction Service No. ED 422 119)

Shoffner, M. F., & Williamson, R. D. (2000). Facilitating student transitions into middle school. *Middle School Journal, 32,* 47-52.

Swaggart, B., Gagnon, E., Bock, S., Earles, T., Quinn, C., Myles, B. S., & Simpson, R. (1995). Using social stories to teach social and behavioral skills to children with autism. *Focus on Autistic Behavior, 10,* 1-16.

Walker, H., McConnell, S., Holmes, S., Todis, B., Walker, J., & Golden, N. (1988). *The Walker social skills curriculum: The ACCEPTS program.* Austin, TX: Pro-Ed.

Weldy, G. R. (1995, February). Critical transitions. *Schools in the Middle,* 4-7.

Wigfield, A., & Eccles, J. S. (1994). Children's competence beliefs, achievement values and general self-esteem: Change across elementary and middle school. *Journal of Early Adolescence, 14,* 107-138.

Wilde, L. D., Koegel, L. K., & Koegel, R. L. (1992). *Increasing success in school through priming: A training manual.* Santa Barbara, CA: University of California.

Williams, M. W., & Shellenberger, S. (1996). *How does your engine run? A leader's guide to the Alert Program for Self-Regulation.* Albuquerque, NM: Therapy Works.

Winebrenner, S. (2001). *Teaching gifted kids in the regular classroom: Strategies and techniques every teacher can use to meet the academic needs of the gifted and talented.* Minneapolis, MN: Free Spirit Publishing, Inc.

Wing, L. (1981).   Asperger's Syndrome: A clinical account. *Psychological Medicine, 11,* 115-129.

Wood, M. M., Davis, K. R., Swindle, F. L., & Quirk, C. (1996). *Developmental therapy – Developmental teaching* (3rd ed.). Austin, TX: Pro-Ed.

World Health Organization. (1992). *International classification of diseases and related health problems* (10th ed.). Geneva: Author.

Yak, E., Sutton, S., & Aquilla, P. (1998). *Building bridges through sensory integration.* Weston, Ontario: Authors.

Index